Handbook of Medicolegal Practice

Handbook of Medicolegal Practice

Edited by

John P. W. Varian FRCS, FRACS(Orth)
Hand Surgeon, Blackrock Clinic, Co. Dublin, Ireland

Butterworth–Heinemann Ltd
Linacre House, Jordan Hill, Oxford OX2 8DP

 PART OF REED INTERNATIONAL P.L.C.

OXFORD   LONDON   BOSTON   MUNICH
NEW DELHI   SINGAPORE   SYDNEY   TOKYO
TORONTO   WELLINGTON

First published 1991

British Library Cataloguing in Publication Data
Handbook of medicolegal practice.
  1. England. Medicine. Negligence. Law
  I. Varian, J.
  344.206332

  ISBN 0-7506-1238-X

Library of Congress Cataloging in Publication Data
Handbook of medicolegal practice/edited by J. Varian.
    p. cm.
  Includes bibliographical references and index.
  ISBN 0-7506-1238-X
  1. Physicians—Malpractice—Great Britain. 2. Medical
jurisprudence—Great Britain. I. Varian, J.
  [DNLM: 1. Jurisprudence. 2. Malpractice. W 32.6 H236]
KD2960.M55H36 1991
346.4103'32—dc20
[344.106332]
DNLM/DLC
for Library of Congress

Filmset by Bath Typesetting Limited, Bath, Avon
Printed in Great Britain at the University Press, Cambridge

Contributors

Deepak K. Chitkara MB, ChB, DO, FCOphth
North Riding Infirmary, Middlesbrough, UK

W. Bruce Conolly FRCS, FRACS, FACS
Hand Surgeon, Sydney Hospital Hand Unit, Sydney, Australia

Albert T. Day JP, DObstRCOG, MRCGP
The Medical Protection Society, Leeds, UK

Ann F. Dingle MB, ChB, FRCS(Eng.)
Registrar in Otolaryngology, North Riding Infirmary, Cleveland, UK

Michael J. Earley MCh, FRCS, FRCS(Plast)
Consultant Plastic Surgeon, St Vincent's Consultants Private Clinic, Dublin,
Ireland

Maurice R. Hawthorne MB, ChB, FRCS(Ed.), FRCS (Eng.)
Consultant Otolaryngologist, North Riding Infirmary, Cleveland, UK;
Examiner for the Royal College of Surgeons of England; Expert Opinion for
the Medical Protection Society

Eurig T. Jeffreys FRCS, FRCS(Ed.)
Consultant Orthopaedic Surgeon, The Robert James and Agnes Hunt
Orthopaedic Hospital, Oswestry, UK

Nigel C. Keddie MA, FRCS, FRCS(Ed.)
Senior Surgeon, West Cumberland Hospital; Honorary Clinical Lecturer in
Surgery, University of Newcastle upon Tyne, UK

Brian J. Lamont DCH, FFARCSI
Consultant in Anaesthesia and Intensive Care, Beaumont Hospital, Dublin,
Ireland

Bartlet J. McNeela MB, ChB, FRCS, FCOphth
North Riding Infirmary, Middlesbrough, UK

Robert F. Nelson QC
1 Paper Buildings, The Temple, London, UK

Andrew Post
1 Paper Buildings, The Temple, London, UK

E. Malcolm Symonds FRCOG
Professor, Department of Obstetrics and Gynaecology, Queen's Medical Centre, Nottingham, UK

John P. W. Varian FRCS, FRACS(Orth)
Hand Surgeon, Blackrock Clinic, Co. Dublin, Ireland

Contents

Part I
General considerations

1 The medicolegal report

J. P. W. Varian

General considerations

A medicolegal report is a medical report prepared for the purpose of litigation. Occasionally it is made out directly to an insurance company, allowing settlement of a claim before it goes to litigation. The examination of the plaintiff and the subsequent report are to assess the disability arising from the accident or incident in question, to report how the disability arose, and to give a prognosis for the future.

It is a legal document and should be treated with respect. It should be typed on good quality headed notepaper. It will, in all probability, be photocopied and it should, therefore, be typed, if possible, on an electric typewriter with a good clear typeface. It should not be hand-written (Figure 1.1). The report should be concise, that is, as short as possible but still covering the facts. Any one doctor can only report to one side in the dispute — either to the plaintiff's or the defendant's solicitors. It should be remembered that the plaintiff's solicitor, if it is to him one is reporting, may well show the report to the plaintiff. Confidential information provided to the lawyer should therefore be put in a separate letter or conveyed by telephone (Figure 1.2).

Always bear in mind that after any report one may be asked in court to restate and justify the statements made in that report. It is to nobody's advantage to make biased statements in a report, which are then retracted on the steps of the court.

The referral

The referral on behalf on the plaintiff will come either from his solicitor directly, or occasionally, via the plaintiff's general practitioner. It will come from the other side either directly from the employer's insurance company or from the solicitors representing the insurers. Frequently, appointments are made by telephone, but it is best, if possible, to resist these requests and demand a written referral which will hopefully contain the reference number of the case, the date of injury, and any special points or queries to be brought to the attention of the examining doctor. Some solicitors are inclined to forget this important letter if they know they can easily obtain appointments by telephone.

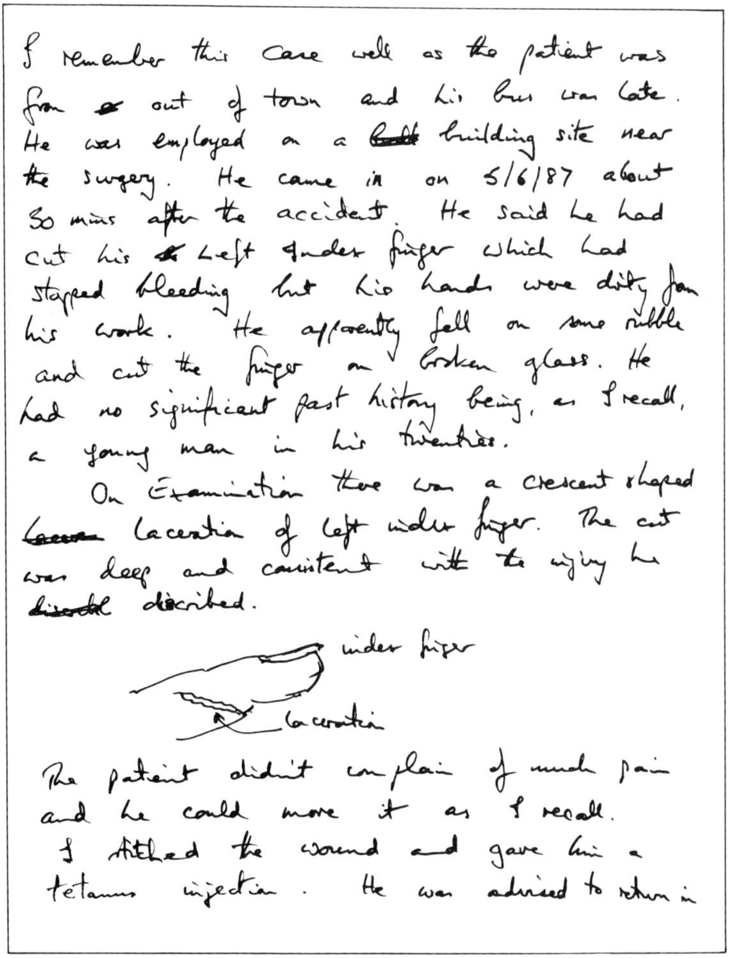

I remember this case well as the patient was
from ~~o~~ out of town and his bus was late.
He was employed on a ~~buil~~ building site near
the surgery. He came in on 5/6/87 about
30 mins after the accident. He said he had
cut his ~~l~~ Left index finger which had
stopped bleeding but his hands were dirty from
his work. He apparently fell on some rubble
and cut the finger on broken glass. He
had no significant past history being, as I recall,
a young man in his twenties.
On Examination there was a crescent shaped
~~lacera~~ laceration of left index finger. The cut
was deep and consistent with the injury he
~~discrbl~~ described.

index finger

laceration

The patient didn't complain of much pain
and he could move it as I recall.
I stitched the wound and gave him a
tetanus injection. He was advised to return in

Figure 1.1 How not to present a medicolegal report

MR JOHN SMITH

Tel   01 880219   1001 Harley Street,
                                         LONDON
                                         20th November 1992

        Re Mrs ABC 32 Ocean View, Birmingham.

Dear Mr XYZ,

I enclose my report on this woman.

You will see from that report that I was not convinced
about the genuineness of her symptoms. Clearly she is
unhappy with the result of her operation and is
maximizing her symptoms to a great degree.

With regard to the question of medical negligence, it is
my opinion that Dr RST did demonstrate a quality of
care less than could be reasonably expected of a man
in his position by failing to make the correct diagnosis,
but the ensuing twelve hour delay in the onset of
treatment did not alter the outcome. It is my opinion,
therefore, that there has been no negligence in this case.

Yours sincerely,

_____

JOHN SMITH

Encl.

Figure 1.2 Example of a letter with confidential information forwarded to a lawyer

Having received the referral letter, the doctor should consider whether he can take on the case. In the United Kingdom it
is common practice for physicians and surgeons to report to

either side on their own patients. However, reporting to the employers or insurers on one's own patient may, on occasions, strain the doctor's loyalty to his patient and he may find himself with a conflict of interest. In some countries it is not considered ethical to report on a patient one has treated to his or her employer's representatives or insurers, after a claim has been made; this produces an adversarial situation.

Plaintiff's work

Most general practitioners like to know that you have examined their patient for a solicitor, and it is a common courtesy to advise the patient to let that doctor know that the examination has taken place. Some solicitors make referrals via the general practitioner so that he is kept in the picture. The medicolegal report should never be copied to the doctor, but a separate letter giving your opinion could be sent if it was requested. The plaintiff may have been treated by another specialist who may, or may not, have already reported to the solicitor. It is wise to liaise with that specialist by telephone, or letter, or through the referring solicitor, as he will have information with regard to the patient's treatment which would be useful. In a complicated case a joint consultation may be necessary. Where the lawyer has not previously asked that specialist for a report, he, the specialist, may be irritated, even to the extent of failing to cooperate with this request. The examining doctor should still, however, make the approach.

Occasionally the patient, for his or her own reasons, will request that other doctors are not informed of the examination; these wishes should be respected. For this reason the patient is seen before consultations with other doctors are carried out.

It is important to remember when reporting to the plaintiff's solicitor that the report may well be shown to the plaintiff. It is also important to remember that a referral from a lawyer gives the examining doctor no mandate to offer the patient advice or treatment.

Defendant's work

In theory, a doctor has no right to examine a plaintiff for an employer or his insurers without the consent of the plaintiff's solicitor or attending physician. However, appointments for such examinations are usually made via the plaintiff's solicitors, so their consent is implied. An offer to consult with the plaintiff's doctor or specialist should be made, but this practice has to a large extent been dropped in the United Kingdom. This should be done prior to the examination date, so that the doctor can attend with the plaintiff if it is considered appropriate. Where a joint consultation is arranged, the venue is a matter for the doctors concerned, but it is usually held at the convenience of the plaintiff's doctor in his or her consulting rooms. These joint consultations have become less common in recent years as they are rarely felt to be necessary, and pressure of work makes them difficult to arrange.

Medical negligence work

Special considerations need to be made with regard to medical negligence cases which, unfortunately, are becoming more common and more prevalent in the western world. This is because, with increasing education and knowledge of their own medical problems, patients have a higher expectation of the results of treatment and are not prepared to accept an element of risk. If a result is less satisfactory than was expected, there is often a feeling that someone was at fault.

Never accept a medical negligence case without first finding out who is involved and what is the substance of the claim. Most doctors prefer to avoid taking on claims against close colleagues. However, nothing is to be gained by turning one's back on all these cases if one is in a position to make useful comment. No sensible lawyer will support a claim for medical negligence without a supporting medical report. Many spurious claims can be stopped, early on, if they are examined by a responsible specialist who can advise that there is no case.

Plaintiffs may be saved considerable expense and bitterness by this course of action. Very often the only thing absent from their management has been an explanation of their unsatisfactory situation, which may not be the fault of any doctor.

The consultation

Many patients are very nervous when attending this consultation, which is different from an ordinary visit to their own doctor, in that much may depend financially on the result of the examination. Some will consciously or subconsciously exaggerate their disability. Aids such as splints tend to be worn for these consultations if they have been prescribed in the past, even though they have not been worn for some time prior to the consultation. The examining doctor should therefore remain observant both before and after the consultation, as well as during it. Many patients are off their guard in the waiting room, especially on their way out, and sometimes demonstrate movements which a few minutes before had been allegedly impossible. The patient's posture, the presence or otherwise of a limp, the quality of a handshake, can all give valuable clues as to real disability. The ability to remove a coat may be significant in shoulder and neck problems. By all means be a gentleman and take the coat, but do not assist in its removal!

It is important to persuade the patient to relax. If one can gain his or her confidence the true state of affairs, which is what the doctor is seeking, will become more apparent. The doctor can then make an impartial, unbiased assessment of disability, which subsequently can be supported in court with authority and confidence. If a relative or spouse wishes to be present, encourage it. Where a child is being examined, a sweet or lollypop usually helps to settle him. Where there is a hand problem it is helpful for that sweet to be wrapped, and while it is being unwrapped a rapid assessment of hand function can often be made. One or two general remarks, followed by the standard initial questions, also give the patient time to relax.

History

History-taking is part of the routine training of all medical undergraduates, and details do not need to be listed here. However, there are some points which are relative to this particular situation. It is important to obtain accurately the patient's first name, marital status, date of birth, occupation and, in upper limb cases, whether he or she is right or left handed. The occasional feminist refuses to give marital status, but the knowledge of this fact may be important in assessing her domestic responsibilities as well as deciding whether she prefers to be addressed as Mrs, Miss or Ms. Date of birth is more useful information than the simple age of the patient, as some hospitals file under date of birth, and it may be useful to have it on record. It may also be relevant to the patient's retirement date. Occupation at the time of injury should be noted, not the occupation at the time of the examination.

A note of the state of the general health of the patient, and any relevant past history, should be taken. Do not fill in pages with lists of conditions from which he or she does not suffer.

A brief history of the injury should be taken. Some solicitors will have advised their clients to say nothing at this stage. The defendant's doctor is, however, entitled to make a judgment whether a disability is consistent with the described injury. When this is explained to the patient he or she usually goes ahead and describes what happened. The doctor should, however, stop the patient going into a long diatribe about whose fault the accident was. The mechanism of injury is all that is required. Details of road traffic accidents should be avoided, but it is sometimes important to know from which direction the plaintiff's vehicle was struck and with what force, in order to assess the mechanism of injury. Whether or not consciousness was lost should be asked, and the state of the patient's memory of the accident.

The injuries should then be listed and checked with the patient. If there are more than two injuries they should be lettered or numbered, one under the other, so that they stand out in the report. All injuries should be listed, although the specialist will confine comments to his or her own specialty later in the report.

Because a court will have to assess compensation for pain and suffering after the injury, it is helpful to include in the report details of how the patient was managed immediately after the injury. In road traffic accidents it should be made clear whether the patient was taken to hospital by ambulance or by car, or whether he or she drove there or went the following day. In factory accidents it is important to know whether the plaintiff was trapped in machinery, and if so for how long. It should be stated whether treatment was given in the works medical centre and/or directly at the hospital and if so, which hospital. Was the person treated and sent home or admitted? If admitted, under whose care was he or she admitted? Did the patient have one or more operations under local anaesthetic or general anaesthetic, and how long was the stay in hospital? Was a splint or use of crutches necessary on leaving hospital? Was physiotherapy and occupational therapy required, and has that treatment been discontinued, or is the person still receiving it? All these points build up a picture of the amount of pain and suffering which the plaintiff had to endure as a result of the accident and which is fully compensatory. Finally, the examining doctor should enquire how long the plaintiff was off work as a result of the injury and whether or not he or she was able to return to his/her pre-accident occupation or to some other job. If the change of occupation was for reasons other than the injury it is important to say so.

All the above information should be obtainable from the patient, parent or guardian. Comparison of that information should be made with that already obtained from other sources, such as the plaintiff's 'Statement of Claim', other specialists' reports, or previous consultation advice. If there are differences in fact, these should be raised with the patient and an attempt made to sort out the truth. Occasionally a patient will admit to a poor memory for the events which may have occurred several years earlier, and this should be noted.

Finally a brief note on the plaintiff's social circumstances should be made if they are relevant.

Present complaints

These should be tabulated and enumerated so that the reader of the report can easily refer to them. It is very easy to alter the import of the complaint unintentionally when noting it down, and certain descriptions are best put in the patient's own words and noted in quotation marks. This particularly applies to descriptions of pain, cosmetic disability, and colour change in the limbs associated usually with cold conditions.

The plaintiff should be allowed to describe personal problems, with regard to continuing disability, without the need for prompting or leading questions by the examining doctor. However, some accident victims can be a little inarticulate and find difficulty in putting into words the problems that they are facing. Most plaintiffs think that the only requirement being asked is a description of problems relating to work, and they have to be prompted to describe any sporting interests or hobbies or musical expertise that may be affected as a result of their disability.

If the plaintiff has not returned to work at the time of the examination a description of the disability, or other reason, that prevents a return to work, should be included in this section.

The examination

During the examination, the examining doctor should confine attention to his or her own field of expertise. The examination must be thorough. Particular attention should be paid to the size and position of the scars, which always loom large in the eyes of courts in the matter of consideration of cosmetic disability. They should be marked on a diagram. If the examiner has any expertise with a camera it is of great assistance to the reader of the report if photographs of the scars can be taken to accompany the report. This is particularly true of scarring involving the face and the hands, and it is even more relevant where the report is for the defendant's solicitors who will not have seen the plaintiff.

There is no difficulty in assessing the disability in a pateint who is relaxed and genuine. The difficulties arise in those plaintiffs who are attempting to maximize their disability or who have an overriding psychological aspect to their complaints. In these cases the doctor must put great reliance on objective tests and treat with some suspicion the disability which is purely subjective. Unfortunately, there is no objective measurement of pain. Sensation is also difficult to assess without the cooperation of the patient although there is now equipment for testing vibration sense in a fingertip similar to that used in audiometry. The genuineness or otherwise of the presence of back pain will always be difficult to assess accurately, as will be the genuineness of a demonstrated grip strength. Each physician will develop his own methods of examination to attempt to elucidate the true state of affairs. One of the simplest is to distract the patient's attention from the part of the body that is being examined. This is sometimes possible when examining the limbs, by either examining two parts of the same limb simultaneously or two sides simultaneously. In the hands note the presence or absence of callosities, or work staining of the palms and fingers.

The written report

General considerations

There are a few important points of technique that will undoubtedly affect the quality of the finished product.

There are two basic methods of recording information obtained from the consultation, depending to some extent on the time allowed for each patient and the quality of secretarial services available. One can take minimal notes and keep the consultation short, allowing time for more patients to be seen;

to do this, either one must record into a dictaphone in the presence of the patient, or the report is dictated immediately afterwards before the next patient is seen. If this is not done, mistakes and omissions will inevitably follow, as one cannot afford to combine a delay in dictating the report with poor note taking. Alternatively full and detailed notes are taken, requiring a longer consultation time. The report can then be dictated days or weeks later, when convenient, either into a dictaphone or directly to a shorthand typist.

There are advantages to both methods. The first deals with the case completely and, by and large, more quickly. However, there is little time for thought and consideration which often add maturity and weight to a report. X-rays, where relevant, will not have been seen, nor other reports studied, and frequently a supplementary report will be necessary later. The second method means a delay before the report goes out, and there always seems to be an infuriating pile of notes waiting to be dealt with which never shrinks. It oftens makes for home-work in the evenings, which is anathema to many doctors. The report, when it appears, however, is usually better balanced and reaches a more profound and considered conclusion. For doctors who do a considerable amount of this work, a dictaphone is essential and it is worthwhile investing in one of good quality.

Consideration should also be given to the other pieces of hardware involved in the production of a report. As already mentioned, a good quality electric typewriter is important. These are rapidly developing into very exotic machines, with their own memory for ease of erasion and automatic standard letters. There is no doubt that a report from one of these computerized machines with both right and left margins and bold typeheadings, looks good and impressive. It undoubtedly adds weight to the opinions expressed in the report. Some doctors use a word processor and printer. The advantage of a computer is its memory, and the ability to insert easily further information into the layout of the report. The author feels that for this work a computerized typewriter is probably the better choice and is considerably cheaper.

Finally, it is very useful to have a small photocopier in the office. Medical records, and other reports that must be returned, can then be rapidly recorded. It also saves the secretary using carbon copies, which are time consuming and less satisfactory in that they in their turn cannot be copied easily.

The layout

The layout described here is the one used by the author, who inherited it from Mr Guy Pulvertaft, who admitted that he learnt it from Sir Reginald Watson Jones. It has a good pedigree therefore, and has proved popular with lawyers in the United Kingdom and Ireland.

Good quality A4 paper should be used, and the heading on the first sheet is printed according to the taste of the doctor. It should not be too loud, and most prefer a conservative design. It should state the doctor's name, usually centrally placed, address and telephone number. This last item can be on the left of the top of the page to balance the address on the right, or put under the address. The doctor may wish to include more than one address, in which case the second one should be on the left. It should be clear, however, in these circumstances, to which address the reader should reply. In the United Kingdom it is not considered ethical to put one's specialty under one's name, but this is common practice in other countries and can be useful where the reader has several reports to sort out from different specialists.

The report, like any legal document, must be dated. This is essential, and it is amazing how often it is omitted. The date should feature prominently, and the best place to put it is in the top right hand corner under the address. Some doctors hide it in amongst the other headings on the top of the page, and some put it at the end with the signature. However, when the report is being sought in a bundle of papers, especially in a hurry under the eye of the judge in court, the most useful and easily seen position for the date is in the top right hand corner of the first page of the report.

The report should start with four main headings. These are

usually put near the top of the first page or they can be put on their own, in the centre of the first page, to make the report look more impressive. These headings are Name, Address, Date of birth, and Occupation (Figure 1.3).

MR JOHN SMITH

Tel   01 880219   1001 Harley Street,
                                             LONDON

                                             20th November 1992

NAME   Mrs ABC

ADDRESS   32 Ocean View, Birmingham

DATE OF BIRTH   12.9.53

OCCUPATION   Process Worker

I examined this woman for the purpose of this report on the 7th November 1992, having to hand a copy of a report by Mr John Taylor, dated 3rd July 1992.

Mrs ABC stated that she is right handed and enjoys good general health.

HISTORY

Mrs ABC stated that on the 3rd April 1992 she was involved in an accident at work wherein ...

Figure 1.3 How to start a medicolegal report

Some doctors add further information as a heading, such as marital status, date of accident, date of admission to hospital, date of report, reference number, etc., but too many confuse the main import of these headings which should be confined to the details of the plaintiff. If one has a reference number of one's own that has to be put on the report, it should be put separately at the top left hand corner of the report, or just under the date.

Report content

The report should deal with the facts as they occurred in chronological order, starting, therefore, with the situation that existed prior to the injury. It can start with a short paragraph noting the state of the patient's general health prior to injury and, for upper limb reports, whether or not the patient is right or left handed. A short note on the patient's social circumstances can be put in at this stage and, if relevant, his or her past history as it affects or may affect the present disability.

History

This is the first of the major sections of the report and is often the longest. It can look tedious and will not make good reading if it is all included in one paragraph (Figure 1.4). Therefore keep sentences short and break it up into several paragraphs.

It is wise to start with the words 'the patient (or plaintiff) stated that' or something similar. If then subsequent information proves to be incorrect, the doctor can avoid being blamed for the inaccuracy. The first sentence should establish the date of the incident or injury and where it happened; whether at work; on the road; in a commercial premises; or in the home.

Examples are as follows:-

Mr X stated that on Friday, 13 April 1979 he was involved in an accident at work wherein ...

MEDICAL REPORT ON JOHN SMITH

HISTORY

Your client John Smith, aged forty-eight years, who works as a milkman, was seen in the Royal General Hospital on the 5th September 1976 as a result of injuries he sustained in a road traffic accident. The circumstances of the accident, as explained to me, were that Mr Smith was walking down a road when he was knocked down by a passing car. He does not think he lost consciousness, and remembers being struck by the car and being thrown to the ground. His memory is then a bit hazy, and the next thing he remembers is being in the Casualty Department of the Royal General Hospital. His initial clinical symptoms consisted of pain and inability to use his left arm, and examination suggested that the shoulder was dislocated. This was confirmed by X-ray examination. At that time, he appeared to have suffered no other injuries. His skull was X-rayed and this showed no fracture. The shoulder was reduced under general anaesthesia and he remained in hospital overnight for observations. He was then discharged with his left arm immobilized in a sling, and he was advised to start exercising it, under the supervision of a physiotherapist, about two weeks later. He was next assessed in the Royal General Hospital on the 3rd October 1976, when he appeared to be making satisfactory progress. He continued to complain of pain in his left arm, and he was noted to have tenderness in the forearm along the line of the radius. Further X-rays were taken, but these showed no fracture of that bone. He complained of some numbness in the arm and hand, and there was also some complaint of stiffness in the neck. The possibility of injury to his brachial plexus, in the root of the neck, could not be excluded. He continued to attend the outpatient clinic and went on to make a satisfactory recovery.

In summary, your client sustained a mild head injury from which he has made a full recovery and a dislocation of the left shoulder. This is recovering well, and he continues to receive physiotherapy. It is a little early to make an assessment of his permanent disability, and I would recommend that this be postponed for a further three months.

Figure 1.4 How not to present a report—no headings, no paragraphs

Ms Y stated that on Saturday, 4 July 1980 she was involved in a road traffic accident wherein . . .

Most patients remember the day of the week that the accident happened more easily than they remember the date.

The history is then set out as suggested in the previous section. The final paragraph should deal with the 'return to work' situation. It is usually of more use to the reader to know how long the plaintiff was off work rather than the date on which the person returned to work, which requires the reader to do some mental arithmetic.

If the plaintiff failed to return immediately to his or her pre-accident occupation it should be stated what work was returned to, and for how long, before resuming the original job.

Present complaints

The medical complaints that the plaintiff has at the time of the examination should be listed numerically. It is useful to list them in the order that they are produced, because it often gives an idea of their relative importance to the plaintiff. The reason why the plaintiff is unable to work should be included, if this is still appropriate. If the information is not volunteered, it should be requested. The final complaint should be a note regarding their ability to follow their sporting interests or hobbies. In the author's experience this information is rarely spontaneously offered unless the plaintiff has a major sporting interest.

Adjectives used to describe pain, emotion and cosmetic change should be quoted exactly and put in quotation marks. However, the anatomical position of a pain or scar should be described in medical terms — the patient usually saying 'it is here' which does not convey much to the reader.

Each complaint should be kept short and précised down to about three lines if possible. Pages of verbatim reporting of what the patient said are unutterably boring and difficult to read.

It is occasionally the case that the doctor is reporting from medical records on a patient who has not been seen for several months. In these circumstances it is wise to put in parentheses, after the heading 'Present complaints', the date when the problems were raised — usually the last visit to the doctor. The same applies to the following section 'on examination'.

Where a follow-up report is being carried out it is really unnecessary to write down all the medical complaints again. The reader will have noted them in the first report, and all that is required in the second report are details of any changes that have occurred in the intervening period. It is useful, therefore, to start with the sentence — 'to take the points as set out in my previous report' — and then go through them numerically. If there is no change, write simply 'no change'. There may, of course, be additional complaints which should be added at the end.

On examination

Examination technique has been discussed in the previous section. Start by stating what has been examined; either a general examination or an examination confined to a special area in which one has expertise. This part of the report can be written in medical terminology and it should be detailed and accurate. It is essential to confine oneself to one's own specialty, and concentrate on reporting the facts. Opinions will come later. Again, try and break up the section into several small paragraphs.

Although this section should essentially be aimed at the doctor for the other side, the lawyers will read it. It should, therefore, be set out so that the lawyer can understand it, and this may involve the occasional term being explained (by two or three words in parentheses). On the other hand, it should not be couched totally in layman's terms which will lack the precision another doctor would like to see.

There is little to be gained by noting masses of negative findings. On the other hand, where the history would lead one to expect a positive finding, the recording that it is absent can be very important. Remember, there is nothing more boring than pages of recorded normality, and the reader may then miss a finding of abnormality in its midst. Verbocity will expand your report but not your medicolegal practice.

It is useful in orthopaedic practice to have printed diagrams for the marking of scars. This can save considerable written description and they are more easily visualized by the reader. The diagrams, however, should be of good quality. Some doctors seem determined to convert them to an abstract work of art (Figure 1.5).

A final paragraph should quote the result of any investigations carried out. The most common of these would be an X-ray, but other tests, such as an audiogram or EMG may be relevant.

Opinion and prognosis

This is the most important section of the report. It should start with a short summary in layman's terms of the history and examination – usually achieved in a couple of sentences. This is followed by one's own diagnosis. It is important to remember at this stage, that the report will probably be shown to the other side and must be compiled with that in mind. Comments on documents received, colleagues' opinions, and even the sobriety of the patient, should be made in a separate letter. However, one should not be afraid to remark on your belief in the genuineness of the plaintiff's complaints or examination findings. It is naive to believe that every claim is genuine, but one must be very sure of one's diagnosis before sticking one's neck out. In particular, it is difficult and dangerous to make the jump from unconscious to conscious attempts to mislead – from the hysterical reaction to the malingerer.

Some assessment of disability is essential. This should be as accurate as possible, but may be difficult, and frequently has to be classified as mild, moderate, or severe. In orthopaedic disability affecting the limbs, it can be represented as a percentage loss, and there are guidelines laid down by the

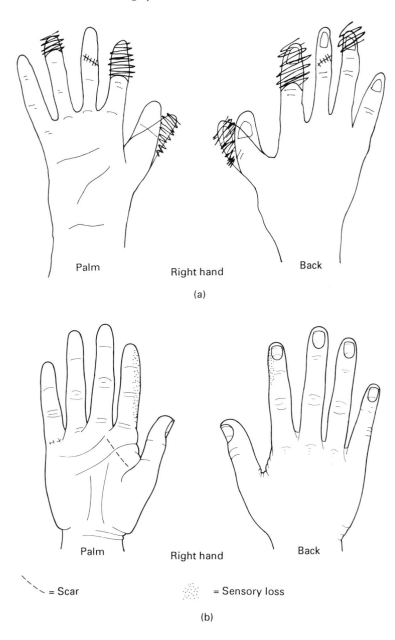

Figure 1.5 (a) How not to do it; (b) how to do it

Department of Health in the United Kingdom and the American Academy of Orthopedic Surgery in the United States (see Appendix 1). At the end of the day, this 'assessed' disability has to be translated into money in the form of compensation. The doctor should be mindful that any attempt to avoid the responsibility of making that assessment, will place the onus on a lawyer or judge, who may be far less qualified to assess the disability. Once the degree of disability is assessed, it is then up to the lawyers to convert that into an appropriate sum of compensation. The doctor should studiously avoid discussing that sum with the patient, who will occasionally try to extract information as to 'what the disability is worth'.

Where a specialist is examining the patient, he may be of the opinion that further treatment, therapy or surgery could reduce the residual disability. The doctor is quite at liberty to raise such an opinion in the report or in a separate letter, but is not entitled to discuss the possibility of further treatment with the plaintiff. The doctor is also entitled to write to the plaintiff's GP giving those opinions so that the GP can consider referring the patient for treatment if so desired. Some would consider such a letter good manners and useful. Others, unfortunately, consider it to be meddlesome and inappropriate and that the specialist, especially if acting for the employer or insurance company, should mind his or her own business. There is no doubt that it can sow in the mind of the patient the seed for thought that previous treatment has been inadequate, once he or she becomes aware that such a letter has been written.

If the plaintiff has not returned to work or has returned to a different, possibly lighter, occupation, it is essential that this be discussed. A clear opinion as to the patient's fitness to return to his or her pre-accident occupation must be given. If still unfit, the reasons to support this statement should also be noted. Some idea should be given as to when the person might become fit to return to that work, if ever. If that person is still off work but the examining doctor believes him to be fit, the lawyer will wish to know when the person became fit for work. This is often impossible to state with any accuracy, but a rough estimate can usually be made. The greatest difficulty in assessment arises when the disability is sufficiently severe to prevent, permanently, return to the pre-accident occupation, but clearly the plaintiff is fit to do something. Unless it is anticipated in the report, the inevitable question will be asked – 'what sort of work can this man do?'. An example of this type of assessment is shown in Appendix 2.

Finally, with regard to disability assessment, there is the question of what to do if the patient's condition is not yet stabilized and the disability is changing. Further surgery may be being planned. In these circumstances, there is no point in making an assessment and the report should be terminated with the suggestion that a further assessment be made in six months. In practice there is little point in making that period of time any shorter, and often a longer wait would be more appropriate. However, even if the disability is changing, it is often helpful to give the referring lawyer some idea as to whether the eventual disability is likely to be large, small or nil.

Next one must deal with the prognosis. For this one needs a crystal ball, and failing that one must do one's best based on standard medical teaching, past experience and common sense. One is prognosticating mainly with regard to the chance of the development of late complications. The most common of these are the risk of osteoarthritis after joint injury, epilepsy after brain injury, contracture after burns, chest problems after inhalation injury, and possibly malignancy after accidental irradiation.

One may be questioned on the chance of late improvement following brain injury, spinal injury or peripheral nerve injury such as brachial plexus injury.

The risks of late problems or the chances of late improvements are recognized in certain situations. However, each plaintiff is individual and warrants individual consideration. By and large, the doctor is wise to avoid giving chances in percentage terms and should stick to four well tried groupings – no risk, possible, probable, and certain. In court one is rarely asked to be more specific and if pushed, one can always plead that one does not have a crystal ball!

Signing off

How does one end the report? Avoid the temptation to try to ingratiate oneself with the reader in Uriah Heep fashion with the sentence 'I hope this is satisfactory and if there is anyway I can help, please let me know' (Figure 1.6). This is weak and lacks authority, undermining the strength of the whole report. If a lawyer does need to seek the doctor's clarification on one or more points he or she will certainly do so, without the invitation.

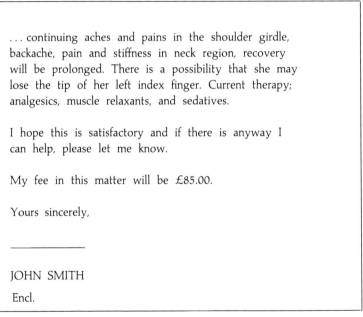

... continuing aches and pains in the shoulder girdle, backache, pain and stiffness in neck region, recovery will be prolonged. There is a possibility that she may lose the tip of her left index finger. Current therapy; analgesics, muscle relaxants, and sedatives.

I hope this is satisfactory and if there is anyway I can help, please let me know.

My fee in this matter will be £85.00.

Yours sincerely,

JOHN SMITH
Encl.

Figure 1.6 How not to conclude a medicolegal report

Do not put your fee at the end of the report. It is amazing how often this is done, presumably to save the price of a piece of paper. It looks most unprofessional. The report will be copied and sent to various parties, including other doctors, and it should not carry the amount of one's fee with it (Figure 1.6).

The report must be signed by the examining doctor. It is a legal document and it is insufficient for one's secretary or other staff to 'p.p.' it in one's name. The best way to finish a report is to say no more after the prognosis. Just stop. There should be no 'Yours faithfully' etc. The name and address and (most important) reference of the person to whom the report is being sent should appear to the bottom left of the page and one's signature with name and qualifications to the bottom right or centre.

2 Court work
J. P. W. Varian

'The con'
'The hearing'

'The con'

A consultation, prior to the court hearing, may be called by the barrister in charge of the case. This usually involves, in a defendant's case, the representative of the insurance company, the solicitor, the doctor or doctors who have examined the plaintiff, and possibly the engineer, who has examined the scene of the accident. In a plaintiff's case, the plaintiff himself may or may not be present in the place of the representative of the insurance company.

The purpose of this meeting is for the barrister to clarify his or her knowledge of the case, hear what the expert witnesses will say in court in response to examination and cross examination, and plan strategy with regard to the court hearing and possible settlement in the intervening period. A good barrister will try to avoid asking questions in court to which he or she does not know the answer, and this is the time to find out the answers. It is a time to clarify medical terminology used in the report, and also to comment on reports from the other side, if they have been exchanged.

From the doctor's point of view, absolute honesty is essential at this stage, and, if he or she sees a weakness in the argument or conclusions, which may come out under cross examination, it should be pointed out.

The vast majority of claims are settled prior to this stage. In most of the straightforward injuries, no 'con' is necessary even if the case is going to court, other than a few words in the antechamber before going into the court room. It is only where there is a dispute on medical evidence that a 'con' is usually necessary, and many of these cases are about medical negligence or cases involved with work-related conditions and diseases, rather than simple injury.

'The hearing'

The consultant should look the part. In front of a jury, the consultant's evidence will carry more weight and, where there is no jury, the judge will be better disposed towards a witness who clearly shows some respect for the court. This involves wearing sober clothing and appearing reasonably well groomed.

Some knowledge of the layout of the court is necessary, and if a doctor is appearing in court for the first time it is important to arrive early, so as to meet the instructing solicitor and counsel before the case starts. If, however, as sometimes happens, the consultant is called after the case has started, it may be necessary to enter court alone. The consultant should then know where to go so that he or she does not accidentally sit with the jury! This sort of mistake tends to disturb the court's concentration and can upset the judge somewhat. The consultant should find a seat amongst those reserved for witnesses, and try to catch the eye of his or her own solicitor to indicate arrival. There is a fine balance between making enough noise to cause one's solicitor to look up and notice one's presence, and making too much noise, so that the judge becomes displeased. In a long case, particularly where there is a dispute of medical evidence, the barrister may prefer the doctor to sit in the next row, in order to enable notes to be passed during the case, particularly during the cross examination of the doctor for the other side.

If it is the hope and expectation of the doctor to leave as soon as he or she has given evidence, this must be agreed with the solicitor before being called. The consultant cannot, however, leave the court until given leave to do so by the judge. In a court case, the plaintiff's case is put first and the plaintiff's doctor is usually called to the witness box immediately after the plaintiff has given his evidence. If the doctor is appearing for the defence, he or she may have to wait until all the plaintiff's witnesses have been heard. However, most judges, if asked by the defendant's counsel, will allow the defendant's doctor to be heard immediately after the plaintiff's doctor, in order to let them both get away.

When a doctor goes to the witness box, he or she is entitled, as an expert witness, to take accompanying notes. It is essential, however, that these notes assist rather than hinder the doctor. They should be contained in a folder and be well ordered. The author has observed doctors take the stand with notes flying and falling in disarray, and the doctor becoming extremely flustered before even being asked his or her name. The notes should be in good order, with the copy of the doctor's report or reports on the top. There is no point when asked to refer to a particular date in his report, as he will inevitably be asked, to have to dive into a big pile of papers trying to find it, muttering that it is there somewhere.

The first thing the consultant will be asked to do is to take the oath. This should be done clearly and crisply and should sound as though it has been done before. The consultant then has to state his or her name. This is normally followed by details of qualifications and place of work. It is not expected that this will be answered with the doctor's curriculum vitae, but the court needs to be given some idea of one's standing in one's profession and one's experience. It is better, however, to allow one's counsel to ask further questions about one's background, rather than trot out more than is required.

The subsequent examination by one's own counsel should not pose any problem. One should be prepared for the questions that will be asked and the answers should be ready. Remember, however, that evidence to a jury should be clear, simple, and easily understood. Do not mumble and rely on a microphone. Remember that frequently the judge, as well as the court's stenographer, is taking down what one says verbatim. Therefore one should allow pauses, and watch the judge's pen out of the corner of one's eye to make sure that he or she is keeping up with what is said.

It is during the cross examination that any witness is put to the test, and the expert witness is no exception. In the author's experience everything is fair in love, war and the courtroom. Barristers, who are very friendly outside the courtroom, will do their best to discredit the opposing witness and his or her evidence. This happens less where there is no jury present, as judges tend not to be impressed by attempts to debase a professional expert witness. However, from the doctor's point of view it is important not to be rattled. Keep in the back of your mind that you know more medicine than the unfriendly lawyer will ever know. Remember that the expert's opinion, provided it is based on a good examination and logical deduction, can rarely be shaken. Where two medical opinions differ, it is for the jury or the judge to choose and prefer one or the other. It is important, however, to voice an opinion and stick by it.

Although it is important to be firm and composed in the witness box, one should not go to the other extreme and try to debase the lawyer. The author has observed a medical witness, a psychiatrist, when asked to clarify a point, say 'I have already answered that question. Watch my lips and I'll say it slowly'. This sort of attitude is unprofessional and loses the sympathy of both judge and jury.

Be careful not to stray outside your own field of expertise. It is tempting to answer questions or give opinions on aspects of multiple injuries that are not in one's own specialty. You can be sure that there is probably another specialist, waiting to be called, who will be likely to trip you up and speak with greater authority. The whole of your own evidence is then weakened. A simple answer to a question in these circumstances is 'that is outside my field of expertise and I would prefer not to comment'.

In a difficult case it is useful to have a note of a couple of references up one's sleeve. No-one expects a doctor to know the whole medical literature on a subject, and if the unfriendly barrister says 'are you acquainted with the work published by Dr X in the Arctic Journal of Tropical Medicine?' then one can answer 'no but Mr Y in the Equatorial Journal stated in 1902. . .'

After cross examination the witness may be re-examined by his or her own lawyer on any points made by the other lawyer. This is usually limited to one or two points of clarification or, where the witness has been demolished, the lawyer may try to repair some of the damage.

The judge may then ask the witness a few questions if necessary, and where there is a material difference in the evidence of the two sides, particularly of alleged medical negligence, the judge may ask an expert whether it is possible to reconcile the two views in any way. An example is where relatives have misunderstood the treatment a patient has received, and subsequently given evidence perceiving negligence where none existed. An explanation of the misunderstanding can often settle the problem for the judge. It is unfortunate that it often takes a court of law to explain such a misunderstanding.

That should conclude the doctor's appearance in court and he or she is usually given permission by the judge to leave the court, if it is desired.

3 The lawyer's view

R. F. Nelson and A. Post

Lawyers, like doctors, are prone to categorization. A potential plaintiff must show that his case is within one of a number of legal formulae, known as 'causes of action', if he is to succeed. The 'cause of action' that is most often relevant to doctors in the course of litigation is negligence.

To establish negligence the plaintiff must show three things: 1. The existence of a duty of care. 2. A breach of that duty. 3. Damage flowing from that breach.

A *duty of care* is a legal obligation to take care for the safety of those who are foreseeably likely to be affected by one's actions. A common example is the duty a motorist owes, to other road users, to take care not to injure them or damage their property. The duty is not an absolute one, but a duty to take reasonable care.

Breach of duty occurs where a person, who owes a duty of care, falls below the standard set by the law. That standard is the standard which would be adhered to by a prudent and reasonable person. In the case of a motorist the standard required is that of the reasonable and prudent motorist, and a driver who does not take the precautions that a reasonable individual would take will be held to have been in breach of duty.

Damage, in law can mean damage to the person or to property. It does not matter that an injury is not really capable of being valued in monetary terms, for the law applies its own rather arbitrary calculus to ascertain the value of the loss of a limb, or the onset of a disease. On the other hand, there are limits on the damage for which compensation is recoverable. Damages cannot be recovered in respect of mere hurt feelings, or shaking-up and upset, that do not amount to a recognized psychological injury.

A plaintiff must demonstrate all three elements to make out a cause of action. To turn to medicine, a doctor owes a duty of care to his or her patient; indeed it has been said that there is an overriding duty to act in the best interests of the patient (*Sidaway* v. *Bethlem Royal Governors*). It is not, however, enough for a patient to show that he or she has suffered harm while within the charge of a doctor who owes that person a duty of care. It must also be shown that the doctor has acted in breach of that duty of care in some respect. So too, if a doctor has acted in breach of a duty of care that he or she owes, but the patient does not suffer any loss in consequence of this, the patient has not made out the cause of action of negligence. A rather dramatic example of this last principle is the case of *Barnett* v. *Chelsea and Kensington Hospital Management Committee*. A night watchman and two colleagues attended the casualty department of a hospital and complained of vomiting after drinking tea. The nurse on duty telephoned a doctor, who told the men to go home and go to their own doctors in the morning. Later that day, the night watchman died of arsenic poisoning. It was held that the doctor had been in breach of duty, but that even if he had examined and treated the man this would not have been enough to save his life. Therefore, it had not been shown that the doctor's breach of duty had made any difference, or caused any harm, and the claim failed.

This doctor had, in the ordinary use of the word, been negligent. As a matter of law, on the other hand, negligence had not been proved because a *necessary* ingredient of negligence is damage caused or materially contributed to by the breach of duty. This breach of duty had made no difference to the outcome (*Hotson* v. *East Berkshire AHA*).

As well as being liable in negligence, a doctor may be liable in contract. It is possible for a doctor to agree to bring about a particular result, and if a doctor was to do this and fail to bring about the result, he or she would be in breach of contract. However, it is a very rash doctor who is willing to guarantee success, and therefore in most claims for breach of contract the breach consists in failing to exercise the skill and care that ought reasonably to be expected, and that breach is in practical terms indistinguishable from negligence.

It is also possible for a doctor to be liable for trespass to the person if a patient is treated without properly obtained consent.

Duty of care

A doctor owes a duty of care to all patients who are treated. This duty is independent of any contract between the doctor and the patient, and applies to a doctor who gives his or her services gratuitously and voluntarily, for example at the scene of an accident or disaster.

A duty may also be owed to third parties, such as persons who might be affected by a failure to treat or deal properly with someone suffering from an infectious disease. A duty will also arise when a doctor writes a report on a patient for the benefit of a third party such as an insurance company.

A Health Authority is vicariously liable for the acts and omissions of its employees, and can also owe a direct duty of care to provide adequate staff and resources as ruled by the Court of Appeal in *Wilsher* v. *Essex AHA*. As from January 1990, Health Authorities became fully financially responsible for doctors working at their hospitals. Whether this will lead to the speedier resolution of medical negligence cases remains to be seen. It does, however, remove disputes between Health Authorities and doctors' medical defence bodies as to how liability should be apportioned.

Standard of skill and care

As stated above the normal standard imposed by the law is that of the reasonable and prudent person. However, doctors, like other professional men and women, are expected to display a higher standard. A doctor must not fall below the standard of an ordinary, competent doctor. As long ago as 1838 it was held that a doctor must bring to his patients 'a fair, reasonable and competent degree of skill' (*Lamphier* v. *Phipos*).

One thing that will be apparent is that since the standard expected of a doctor is dependent on the standards of other doctors, so as practice and knowledge develop, so the standard of care will change. A case that illustrates this is *Roe* v. *Minister of Health*. A spinal anaesthetic was kept in glass ampoules stored in phenol solution. The container was knocked over and the solution contaminated the anaesthetic through invisible cracks. The risk of penetration through invisible cracks was one that was unknown at the time that the anaesthetic was administered in 1947. In 1951 a book was published which drew attention to this risk. It was held that the doctor had not been negligent, but the court added that if the same mistake had been made after 1951, the doctor would have been negligent.

A doctor who practises a particular specialization is expected to show the skill of the reasonably competent exponent of that specialization. Lord Scarman said in *Maynard* v. *West Midlands HA* that 'a doctor who professes to exercise a special skill must exercise the ordinary skill of his specialty'.

The standard of skill and care expected of a doctor depends on the position held by that doctor, not on age or experience. Inexperience is no defence to an allegation of medical negligence. A young or inexperienced doctor can, however, discharge his or her duty by seeking the advice and help of a superior (*Wilsher* v. *Essex AHA*).

The Bolam test

While it is easy enough for a judge to establish the standard of care expected of a reasonable and prudent driver, the standard of care expected in the field of medical negligence presents more difficulties. There can be honest differences of opinion as to diagnosis and treatment. There may be different schools of thought as to the proper treatment of a particular condition. It would be very difficult, and would certainly not be desirable, for a judge to attempt to lay down proper medical practice in a particular situation.

The solution to this difficulty that is favoured by the law is to say that a course of conduct will not be negligent if it is one which would have been followed by a body of respectable medical opinion; even if it would not have been followed by a majority of medical opinion. The best known expression of this approach is in the case of *Bolam* v. *Frien Hospital Management Committee*, and the test is known as the Bolam test. In that case the plaintiff had suffered fractures during the course of electro-convulsive therapy. He complained, *inter alia*, that relaxant drugs had not been used. The use of relaxants had significant side-effects; some practitioners used them and some did not. The judge directed the jury that a doctor:

> is not guilty of negligence if he has acted in accordance with a practice adopted as proper by a responsible body of medical men skilled in that particular art.
>
> (*Bolam* v. *Frien HMC*)

The Bolam test has been applied to all areas of medicine: diagnosis, treatment, disclosure of risks of treatment and even most recently the question of what treatment is in the best interest of the patient (*In Re F*, 1989). Medical negligence actions are no longer tried by a judge and jury but by a judge alone; this makes no difference to the application of the test.

Breach of duty

Almost the entire range of medical activity can give rise to allegations of medical negligence. It may, however, be useful to look at a few examples as evidence of the court's approach.

Negligence may consist in failure to examine or to diagnose, as in the case of *Barnett* v. *Chelsea and Kensington Hospital Management Committee* discussed above.

Negligence may consist in an error of diagnosis, as in *McCormack* v. *Redpath Brown & Co Ltd*, where the plaintiff was examined by a doctor after receiving a blow on the head. The doctor failed to discover a hole of one-quarter to one-half inch in diameter, and this was held to be negligent. If the condition is a rare one it is more likely that a failure to diagnose it will not be negligent. In *Hulse* v. *Wilson* the doctor failed to diagnose cancer of the penis in a young man. The condition was rare in a young patient, and it was therefore held that the defendant had acted reasonably in thinking that the plaintiff was suffering from venereal disease. However, if a doctor is faced by symptoms which he or she does not recognize, then a colleague with greater experience should be consulted or the patient should be referred to a specialist.

Negligence is most frequently alleged where there is said to have been an error in the course of treatment. If the plaintiff is to succeed he must satisfy a double test; it must be shown both that the defendant has made a mistake, and that the mistake is one that a reasonably careful and skilful doctor would not have made. It is obvious that things can go wrong, particularly in the course of an operation, without any mistake having been made. However, it is also important to recognize that a careful doctor may make a mistake when carrying out a difficult treatment or operative procedure, without necessarily being in any way negligent.

This is illustrated by two cases involving the administration of injections. In *Calderia* v. *Gray* the needle was misplaced and struck the sciatic nerve and this was held to be negligent. In contrast in *Williams* v. *North Liverpool Hospital Management Committee* an injection which should have been made into a vein in fact was made into tissue. There, it was said that the vein had been difficult to find and, in those circumstances the mistake had not been negligent.

An area of considerable recent concern has been the question of warning patients about the consequences and risks of treatment. The question of whether the warning given by a doctor is proper or not is to be decided according to the Bolam principles, and therefore the test is whether a respectable body of medical opinion approves of a warning in the form given. This was settled in the case of *Sidaway* v. *Governors of Bethlem Royal Hospital*, in which attempts to introduce North American principles of informed consent into the English law proved unsuccessful. The contents and form of a proper warning will vary from case to case, and in particular will depend on the state of the patient.

Proof of medical negligence

The standard proof applied by the English courts, in civil matters, is that a matter is to be proved on the balance of probabilities. This applies not only to matters of liability, but also to the consequences of a negligent act or omission.

It may be impossible to say for certain whether a particular complication has been caused by an earlier incident, but it will still be necessary for the expert to assess and report whether it is more likely than not to have been caused by the earlier incident. The court will wish to decide the matter on the balance of probabilities and a report must take account of that fact, however uncertain causation or prognosis may actually be.

The burden of proving both negligence and the causative link between that negligence and the injury sustained, rests on the plaintiff. In some cases the link may properly be inferred from the evidence, but where a plaintiff can only show that his or her injury had any one of several possible causes, some innocent and one due to the doctor's breach, the claim will not succeed. Thus, in *Wilsher* v. *Essex AHA* the plaintiff could prove that his retinal condition was caused by any one of a number of different agents, but had not shown that one of those, namely the defendant's failure to prevent excess oxygen being administered to him in the special care baby unit, was in fact the cause. Hence he had failed to discharge the burden of proof as to medical causation, and on the facts of that particular case a re-trial was ordered.

There is no authority in English law at present for the proposition that a plaintiff can recover damages for the lost chance of a better medical result which might have been achieved by prompt diagnosis and correct treatment, if the plaintiff is, in fact, unable to establish a doctor's or Health Authority's breach of duty as the cause of his or her condition.

In *Hotson* v. *East Berkshire Area Health Authority* a thirteen year old boy injured his hip in a fall. The injury was not correctly diagnosed at hospital. The trial judge held that even if the Health Authority's medical staff had correctly diagnosed and treated the plaintiff when he first attended the hospital, there was still a 75% risk of the plaintiff's disability developing. However, the judge concluded that the medical staff's breach of duty had turned that risk into an inevitability, thereby denying the plaintiff a 25% chance of a good recovery and hence entitling him to 25% of the full value of the damages awardable for his disability.

The Court of Appeal affirmed this decision, but the House of Lords held that no assessment of the value of a loss of a chance could arise where the damage complained of had already been sustained, or had become inevitable before the child even went to hospital.

The plaintiff must also prove that the injury suffered was foreseeable. However, this tends to be a task that is not too burdensome in medical negligence actions, as in most cases a doctor can foresee, only too easily, the consequences of an error.

Damages

The claim may include damages for pain, suffering and loss of amenity, financial loss and expense incurred e.g. lost earnings, medical and travelling expenses, and future loss such as the cost of nursing care and continuing loss of earnings. Damages are categorized as general damages or special damages. General damages are damages for pain, suffering, and loss of amenity and all future (post-trial) losses. Special damages are loss and expense already incurred (pre-trial).

The role of the expert

The expert witness may have to give evidence on liability, the cause of the plaintiff's condition and quantum, the degree of disability and loss of amenity on which the amount of compensation will be based. The importance of this role cannot be overstated; the court depends upon the expert's assistance and guidance in a number of crucial respects. The expert can explain technical issues and describe medical procedure. He or she can assist with the sometimes onerous task of transliterating and interpreting medical notes. On liability the expert has to deal with the patient's condition and its cause, with diagnosis and treatment, and has to help the court decide whether the doctor has been negligent. A most important function is to set out proper practice, so that the court can assess whether the defendant complied with this standard. On quantum he or she has to deal with the prognosis of the injury and continuing factors, such as future care, which have financial implications.

An expert is therefore, at least in part, present to assist the court. He or she obviously has an opinion (for that is the very reason for being called) and is entitled, and indeed bound, to press that opinion with all the force that can be mustered. The expert must not, however, allow his or her espousal of a party's cause to detract from the role of being an honest assistant to the court.

In most cases where liability is at issue each side will have one or more experts contending that their own side's case is correct. The course of cross-examination may then become decisive. An expert who, with credibility, can maintain his or her opinions, and is thereby able to convince the judge of their soundness, will probably win a case. Alternatively, an expert who capitulates in cross-examination can fatally weaken his or her side. The balance between sensible concession and capitulation is a matter of experience and expertise.

Rules of court require that the substance of the expert's evidence be disclosed to the other side before trial. The purpose of this rule is to allow the areas of agreement between the sides to be identified in advance, thus saving time at the trial. This is done by way of a report compiled by the expert which is served on the other side.

It is proper for the report to be discussed with counsel and consequently amended. It is not proper for the report to be drafted by one of the lawyers (*Whitehouse* v. *Jordan*). This is a difficult area and borderline cases inevitably arise, but a guideline that may assist is to say that it is proper for a lawyer to affect the organization and scope of the report, but it is not proper for the lawyer to interfere with the actual opinions expressed in the report. The barrister may test the conclusions and discuss them with the expert. He or she may suggest an alternative explanation to the expert, and if the expert is persuaded of the validity of that alternative view it is proper for the report to be amended. What is absolutely crucial is that at the end of this process the expert feels able to defend and justify every word and every implication in the report. If he or she cannot do so the case will be diminished.

It is not proper for an expert to put only part of his or her opinion into the report. What is required is that the substance of the expert's opinion be disclosed (*Ollet* v. *Bristol Aerojet*), and that necessarily requires that all material parts of the expert's opinion should be set out in the report.

It should be added that the expert's role is not restricted to his or her own evidence. The barrister in a case will need to question the expert witness or witnesses called by the other side. That witness may be a specialist of international reputation in his or her own field. If the barrister is to do this effectively, he or she must temporarily acquire sufficient expertise to challenge that expert, and identify and expose any weaknesses in his or her evidence. The knowledge that will allow the lawyer to do this will have been gained from his or her own expert. It is very important that the expert witness should be present during the opposite number's evidence and should be prepared to assist the barrister in the cross-examination by pointing out any possible errors or by identifying areas into which it is likely to be fruitful to enquire. Medical negligence litigation is most effective if the lawyer and the expert witness can work together as a team.

References

Barnett v *Chelsea and Kensington HMC* (1969): 1 QB 428
Bolam v *Frien HMC* (1957): 1 WLR 582–586
Calderia v *Gray* (1936): 1 AER 540
Gold v *Harringay HA* (1987): 2 AER 888
Hotson v *East Berkshire AHA* (1987): 2 AER 909
Hulse v *Wilson* (1953): *BMJ*, **ii**, Oct, 890–891
In Re F (1989): 2 WLR 1025
Lanphier v *Phipos* (1838): C&P 475–479
McCormack v *Redpath Brown & Co.: The Times* 24 March 1961
Maynard v *West Midland HA* (1984): 1 WLR 634–638
Ollett v *Bristol Aerojet* (1979): 3 AER 544
Roe v *Minister of Health* (1954): 2 QB 66
Sidaway v *Bethlem Royal Governors* (1985): 2 WLR 480
Whitehouse v *Jordan* (1981): 1 WLR 247
Williams v *North Liverpool HMC: The Times* 17 January 1959
Wilsher v *Essex AHA* (1987): QB 730

Part II
Medical negligence

4 General principles

W. B. Conolly

The average doctor has no real understanding of medical negligence or malpractice. He or she unwittingly causes a patient to begin a claim, or unintentionally helps the patient to prosecute a claim. The doctor makes unnecessary mistakes prejudicial to his or her defence. This chapter aims to provide guidelines for the doctor who may be the defendant in a medical negligence action. This chapter also provides guidelines for the doctor who may be called as an expert witness for the plaintiff or a defendant in such a case.

The history of medical negligence/malpractice

The first laws mentioning malpractice were probably those outlined in the code of Hammurabi (Lyons and Petrucelli, 1979). Punishments for failure of treatment are written in this code.

> If a doctor has treated a man for a severe wound with a metal knife and has caused that man to die, his hands shall be cut off.

The severe punishments for a physician's failures listed in the code (such as cutting off the hand) should be matched against the punishments, which could include execution, meted out for the failure of other professions and the transgressions of one person against another. If in those days, a man destroyed the eye of a patrician, his own eye would be destroyed. One may wonder whether, under the risk of such stringent penalties, any practitioner would have had the nerve to perform an operation, but it may well be that the code was not enforced to the letter. In classic Greek culture, Plato held that actions of physicians should be judged only by other physicians. Aristotle, his pupil, emphasized that the only penalty applicable to any wrong doing by a physician was limited solely to injury of his reputation and to nothing else (Thompson, 1910).

In English law, the first recorded decision concerning civil liability of a surgeon was an action brought against J. Mort, a surgeon, in 1374. This involved the treatment of a patient who had an injured hand. The defendant was held not to be liable, on the basis of a legal technicality. In any event, the court ultimately ruled that if negligence could be proven by such a patient, the law would provide a remedy. The court further held that if the surgeon does as well as reasonably possible, and employs all due diligence to the cure, it is not right that he should be held culpable.

In 1423, the joint College of Physicians and Surgeons in London produced the ordinance against malpractice, which required a surgeon to report all patients who were desperately ill, within three days. The first liability case in the United States of America was filed in 1794. The husband of a deceased woman sued because of alleged negligence during a mastectomy operation (Sabiston, 1989). The doctor was found liable. In 1866, Dr J. Elwell, a Professor of Criminal Law at the Western Reserve University, wrote a medicolegal treatise on Malpractice and Medical Evidence (Elwell, 1866). Prior to 1885, doctors in the United Kingdom had to arrange their own defence and bear the cost themselves. If they were victims of slander or libel, they had to sue their prosecutor themselves or suffer in silence.

The Medical Defence Union

The Medical Defence Union of the United Kingdom was founded in 1885. For the first thirty five years the subscription was ten shillings and this covered advice, defence, provided lawyers and paid their fees. In the 1920s members were indemnified against all costs of defence, and partially against excessive plaintiff's costs and damages. By 1930, all legal costs and damages were paid. In 1947, the union began to provide members with services through a network of lawyers in every main city in the world except in the United States of America.

The Medical Protection Society

In 1892, the London and Counties Medical Protection Society was formed from dissatisfied members of the Medical Defence Union. Later this society became known simply as The Medical Protection Society. Today, the MDU and MPS assist members in matters of professional principle and provide advisory, preventative and educational services, as well as compensation for patients damaged by negligence. Each has an experienced permanent medical staff.

Causes of complaints and actions against doctors

Complaints are caused by misdiagnosis and poor quality of care, but most complaints are about the behaviour of, and communication with, doctors and not their technical incompetence. Failure of communication is by far the most common complaint. The best medicine involves a successful doctor–patient relationship, and this depends on the doctor having the art of listening and speaking to patients. The failure of communication may also be between the doctor and the medical and paramedical staff.

The failure of doctor/patient communication

The three common complaints by patients are that:

1. The doctor fails to listen to what the patient is saying about personal circumstances and illness.
2. The doctor fails to explain to the patient in simple and clear terms what is the diagnosis, what treatment is recommended, and what are the risks of that treatment.
3. The doctor fails to discuss the complication or unsatisfactory result. Most patients are not seeking compensation, but a frank explanation of what went wrong. A defensive attitude by the doctor causes anxiety and resentment and this as much as anything leads to litigation.

Failure of the doctor/patient communication may occur at the initial consultation or later in the hospital. It may involve the consent, leading to the patient pleading later that he did not understand what he was signing. Postoperative instructions may be poorly explained or not understood. Discussion with relatives can lead to misunderstandings.

Failure of communication between the doctor and the medical and paramedical staff

This failure of communication may involve written notes or reports or telephone contact. Most of the problems occur in the Accident and Emergency Department, and the other problems occur in the handing over of shifts at nights and weekends. Problems often occur when a doctor, in charge of a case, goes on holiday or overseas. It is his or her job to ensure that a locum has sufficient experience and sufficient knowledge of the case.

When a consultant delegates to a registrar, it is his or her responsibility to be sure that the registrar has sufficient experience to carry out the job and the consultant must be available for supervision as necessary.

It is the responsibility of the doctor requesting a report, such as an X-ray or pathology report, actually to see that X-ray or report.

Prevention of complaints arising from poor communication

1. Strive for an excellent doctor/patient relationship at all times. Courtesy, consideration, and communication, are vital in achieving this end.
2. Take seriously patients' suspicions or feelings and wherever possible follow their suggestions or requests. For instance, if a mother is anxious for her son's hand to be X-rayed, it is best to follow that request.
3. Avoid 'off the cuff' criticisms of another doctor or hospital.
4. Answer telephone calls and letters from patients.
5. Seek the help of interpreters when there are language difficulties.
6. Keep and check clinical records. Make them legible. Remember that one day, in the future, your case record may be reviewed in court.
7. Keep up to date on safety regulations. Do not ignore

Department of Health circulars concerning the law and patients, especially relating to drugs.

8. Check and supervise medical and nonmedical subordinates, especially concerning follow-up arrangements.

Doctor as defendant

What to do when an incident occurs

An 'incident' is any event that suggests the possibility of a malpractice lawsuit.

If a doctor suspects the possibility of a medical negligence matter, no matter how unreasonable, that doctor should notify the relevant defence body immediately. Initially this can be done by telephone, but it must then be put in writing. An incident report should be prepared. This should be a plain statement of the facts without any comment or expression of opinion. It should all be typed and signed. This report should be addressed to the defence union, for the attention of the legal advisers. Copies of the report should not be filed in the patient's casenotes, but retained in the doctor's secure personal files. Such reports may be legally privileged documents. The report should be a plain narrative statement of the facts without comment, opinion or speculation.

Situations which may alert one to the possibility of a medical practice law suit

1. The patient or a member of the family may express dissatisfaction with the care given by the doctor, or there may be a complication or an unanticipated bad result.

2. There may be a request for medical records by the patient, another doctor or a solicitor. If this occurs, never send the original records and always demand written authorization, from the patient, before any information is released.

3. There may also be contact from a solicitor requesting information on the patient's treatment.

4. Failure of a patient to keep scheduled follow-up visits or failure of a patient to pay an account may also make one suspect a law suit is intended.

The subsequent report

Later a full report may be requested by the defence organization. This needs the most careful attention and trouble, and the following details are advised for inclusion.

The doctor

1. Name, address, qualifications and current appointments.
2. A curriculum vitae for those in training posts.

The patient

1. Full name, age, gender and occupation.
2. The names and appointments of other practitioners involved in the case.
3. Details of the member's personal involvement and dealings with the patient – symptoms, signs, investigations and treatments as a narrative of fact.
4. Photocopies of the relevant clinical records with the authors of entries identified.
5. Details of membership of the defence union.

The case notes

1. At this stage, the doctor should ensure that all case notes are fully written up, and not tampered with at a later date. Any retrospective entry should be clearly marked and dated.
2. Check that pieces of equipment, fractured needles or X-rays are safely kept. X-rays must be dated and labelled R or L side. Seek advice from the defence union before replying to a request for reports from any interested party.

3. Maintain, as far as possible, an amicable relationship with the patient and arrange whatever follow-up treatment is necessary.
4. Make contemporaneous written notes of all oral communications with the patient, or the patient's family, concerning the incident.
5. Do not casually discuss treatment of the patient with anyone except the defence union or appropriate medical consultants.
6. If records are requested send copies and never the originals.
7. Save all correspondence regarding the incident in a separate file from the patient's medical record. Include a list of all records that have been provided, and all notes or oral communications concerning the incident.
8. Become a medical educational resource for your defence team.
9. Review text books and medical articles relating to medical issues in the case. Conduct a Medline search if possible. Educate your defence team about the strength and weakness of your case. They must know about the drifting view points and alternative treatments.
10. Stay calm and try and avoid surprise, anger, panic and self doubt. Be honest and do not try to hide any facts. To remain level headed is essential in preparing any successful defence.
11. Try and arrange a meeting with your legal advisers as soon as possible.

The importance of medical records

The lawyers of medical defence bodies spend their time endeavouring to defend that which appears, or perhaps more frequently, that which does not appear in medical records. The doctor's qualitative care is often judged by the quality of his notes, and this becomes even more important when one realizes that it may take some years for the case to come to court. Weak notes mean weak defence, and no notes may mean no defence.

Medical records should be clear, concise, comprehensible and capable of being read out in court.

Notes which have been altered can lead to a loss of credibility in court. Records which have been tampered with may render a case indefensible.

What are the lawyer's responsibilities to the defendant?

The lawyer should:

1. Keep you informed about litigation procedures.
2. Explain the significance of each stage of the proceedings.
3. Thoroughly prepare you for your role in the proceedings.
4. Carefully investigate and prepare the case by deciding strategy, tactics and the means to defend you.
5. Evaluate all the factors which could win or lose the case for the defence.

This last point would depend on the status of the medical records; the seriousness of the injury and potential loss; the appearance and credibility of the plaintiff; the defendant and the expert witnesses. The calibre of the judge, jury, and legal advisers and the previous results of similar cases are all relevant.

Frequent communication between you and your lawyer is essential. You must make your lawyer completely knowledgeable about the case, and you must be comfortable with his or her approach to your defence.

Outcome of the complaint or action

The case may be defensible, indefensible or doubtful. Many more cases are settled than are contested to a conclusion. A settlement is an agreement made between the parties to an incident, claim or law suit that resolves their legal dispute. A settlement is a financial disposition of the case without a decision on the merits. Mostly payment is made to the plaintiff in exchange for a release. This legal document absolves the defendant from all past, present and future liability in connection with the incident. Most releases specifically state that the settlement by the defendant is not an admission of fault.

Many cases are settled out of court because:

1. The patient is fully justified and the doctor has no defence.
2. Although the lawyers are convinced of the doctor's innocence, there are gaps in the defence often due to poor records.
3. So many doubtful factors are present that, although the doctor was probably not at fault, the case is settled to avoid the cost of legal expenses.
4. Out of court settlements take place only when there is a serious risk that the case will not be won. Some prefer this, in order to avoid publicity even if their innocence is certain.
5. No settlement is made without the member's consent. If a member insists on going to court the defence body takes his wishes into account.

Factors which may influence the decision of whether to settle a case or not are:

1. Evidence — missing, illegible or altered records, unavailable witnesses.
2. Expert witnesses — lack of expert support for the plaintiff or the defence.
3. Serious damages to the plaintiff.
4. The likely costs.
5. Previous results in such cases.
6. Personality factors concerning the plaintiff, the defendant, the judge, the jury and the lawyers.

The doctor as the expert witness in cases of medical malpractice

A doctor may be asked to be either a *witness to fact*, or an *expert witness*.

Witness to fact

A medical witness to fact is a doctor who has first hand knowledge of the case before the court, and is called to give evidence of the facts which he or she knows. After giving evidence of fact, about the nature and the extent of a physical injury, he may also give a professional opinion about the degree of disablement. He or she does not, however, become an expert witness since the whole evidence given is derived from a knowledge of the facts of the case. He or she must not give evidence relying on skills or experience which are not possessed. A witness to fact may be subpoena'd to attend court.

Expert witness

A doctor who has had no professional responsibility in the case, may agree to give medical evidence. He or she is invited by the parties and not called by subpoena. Usually, the lawyer will first ask the expert for his or her report and if that report appears useful the lawyer will ask the expert to attend court and give evidence. The opinion given should be a detached opinion on the standard of care. The expert witness should confine opinion to his or her own area of expertise and not trespass on another expert's domain, or the function of the judge.

Opinion on the case notes alone

One might be asked for an opinion by the solicitors for the defence organization without actually seeing the patient. There will be a lot of material to read and analyse. If not already done, number each page for cross reference because one will need to read and reread, and make any cross references. Note who was the treating doctor and his or her degree and area of specialization. Note his or her practice environment and the facilities available there. Is he or she in a city teaching hospital, a suburban hospital or a country town miles from anywhere? Note particularly the dates of the injury and the various treatments. It may be advisable to make a chronological timetable as a summary (see p. 142). If two or more doctors are involved in the case, one may probably need to write a separate report on each doctor's participation in the case.

Note carefully the dates of any X-ray or pathology reports, and wherever possible ask to see the X-rays yourself.

Opinion in court

The role of the expert witness for the defence is difficult. He or she must be more credible than the plaintiff's expert witness because he or she must convince the judge or jury that opinions expressed concerning the accepted standard of practice, causation and the propriety of the defendant's treatment are correct − after the jury has heard a contrary expert opinion that explains the plaintiff's injuries (an opinion which the jury heard first). The jurors tend to identify with the patient. The jurors may think the doctor is protecting his or her own 'kind', and therefore there is a credibility burden.

To defeat the opinion of the plaintiff the doctor must be straightforward, unequivocal, clear and above all honest. The whole key to the case is whether there has been any deviation from an accepted surgical practice.

Expert witnesses will be selected from those with a similar status and experience, to testify whether a particular doctor's care has been up to the standard of current practice. At the end of the day, it is the judge who decides after hearing the facts and circumstances of the particular case and the opinions of the independent expert witnesses called by each party.

There is a difference between the medical expert taking part, for example, in a clinicopathological conference and the medical expert taking part in the adversarial process of jurisprudence. In the former situation the expert gives his or her best interpretation of the case. He or she does not confirm or dispute the tactics of the treating physician. The medical expert realizes that the clinical manifestations of the biological process, even when scrutinized at the highest levels of medical academic practice, can be confusing and confounding.

In the latter situation the expert may or may not be considered a true authority on the issue at hand. In the adversarial process, the expert is expected to be an ally of either the defendant or the plaintiff. He is not appointed by the court to advise the judge as to the interpretation of the medical evidence. Counsel for both parties carefully select their experts to buttress their particular arguments. If the expert's honest analysis does not support the case put by one of the sides, that expert will not of course be retained, and a new expert whose testimony is more congenial will be sought. Neither party to the dispute wants any surprises, doubts or equivocations from the expert medical witness. Once the testimony for each side has been represented, opposing counsel will attempt to refute the interpretation of the testimony or the credibility of the witness.

Guidelines for the expert witness

The court room is not a classroom, a consultation room or an operation room. Doctors who are accustomed to a particular set of rules, practices and traditions must become acclimatized to new and unfamiliar surroundings and a different set of rules.

Although it may be reasonable for an expert witness to offer a personal opinion in response to a direct question, that opinion must be qualified, to whatever extent necessary, to include the possibilities of important alternative interpretations and approaches. The expert witness may be pressured by counsel to provide unequivocal answers. This pressure must be resisted.

Whatever the merits of the adversarial system, the expert witness is not one of the combatants. The expert's sole allegiance is to the truth and the body of knowledge within his or her area of special competence.

References

Elwell, J. J. (1866) *A Medico-Legal Treatise on Malpractice and Medical Evidence*, Baker, Voorhis and Co., New York

Lyons, A. S. and Petrucelli, R. J. (1979) *Medicine: An illustrated history* — Code of Hammurabi, Macmillan p. 67

Thompson, D'Arcy W. (1910) *The Works of Aristotle*, (Trans) Clarendon, Oxford

Sabiston, D. C. Jr. (July 1989) Professional Liability in the 1980s — Problems and Solutions. *American College of Surgeons Bulletin* **70**, No. 12 p. 6

Selected bibliography

Alton, W. G. (1977) *A Trial Lawyer's Advice for Physicians*, Little, Brown & Company, Boston

American College of Surgeons Bulletin, (May 1977) **72**, No. 5

Dix, A., Errington, M., Nicholson, K. and Powe, R. (1988) *Law for the Medical Profession*, Butterworths, Guildford

Elder, Ian C. (January 1988) Malpractice Suits — Minimising the Risks. *The Australian Family Physician*, **17**, No. 1, p. 35

Hakins, C. (1985) *Mishap All Malpractice*, Blackwell, Oxford

Knight, B. (1982) *Legal Aspects of Medical Practice*, Churchill Livingstone, Edinburgh

Medical Protection Society and the Medical Defence Union, Publications of, London

Taylor, J. L. (1970) *The Doctor & The Law*, Pitman, London

General practice
T. Day

General practitioners deal with the majority of medical problems presented to them without reference to hospital. The doctor is more likely to work in partnership than to be single-handed, and if he or she is working within the National Health Service will work under contract to one or more Family Health Services Authorities (FHSA) or Health Boards (HB) to provide general medical services, normally on the basis of twenty four hour-a-day cover, and thus retain permanent overall responsibility for the patient.

The contractual responsibilities of NHS general practitioners 'Terms of Service' are set out for the doctor in the National Health Service (General Medical and Pharmaceutical Services) Regulations, amendments to which are made from time to time and which are equally binding on the doctor. The NHS general practitioner's remuneration is governed by the Statement of Fees and Allowances, known as 'The Red Book' – which is amended frequently. General practitioners need to be aware of changes in the rules governing their services and payment, and be careful to implement them promptly.

The clinical needs of the patients are met by the doctor(s) working with one or more community nurse, midwife and health visitor, all employed by the Local Health Authority or Health Board. Some practices have the services of other directly-attached staff, working in a variety of fields. Many practices employ their own nurse(s).

Patient care is provided either at home or at the surgery. Surgery premises vary widely, and may be purpose-built or converted, large or small, occupied by one doctor or many. They may be owned by the doctor(s), a third party or the Health Authority/Board. All have to be approved for use in the NHS. The extensive administrative arrangements for dealing with messages, appointments, post in and out, as well as the business side of the practice are the responsibility of the doctor(s), who employ ancillary staff, for example receptionists, secretary, book-keeper, filing clerks and computer operator. The ancillary staff work under the direction of a senior who may be the practice manager. The policies are laid down by the doctor(s), who are responsible for staff not only to the FHSA/ HB, under their contractual terms of service, but also likely to be held vicariously liable for the negligent acts of their employees.

This briefest of work sketches is intended to indicate that general practice has many facets and that from a legal viewpoint there are duties which stem from the professional aspect of practice, those which stem from practice being a business, an employer and one which deals with the public. This book is not intended to encompass the 'business' of medicine and I will simply advise the reader to seek legal advice when partnership deeds are to be drawn up or contracts of employment written, as well as to take professional advice whenever there is an action planned which might have legal implications.

Confidentiality and disclosure of information

The doctor is asked frequently to provide information or an opinion about a patient for a variety of purposes. As a generality, before considering your response, it is worthwhile enquiring of oneself:

1. Who is asking and are they entitled to ask?
2. Has the patient given consent?
3. For what purpose is the information required?

If you are in doubt ask the advice of the professional secretariat of your protection or defence society.

Remember that the secrets you hold are those of your patient, not your own. The General Medical Council provides guidelines in its booklet 'Professional Conduct and Discipline: Fitness to Practise' ('The Blue Book') in which it advises:

It is a doctor's duty strictly to observe the rule of professional secrecy by refraining from disclosing voluntarily to any third party information about a patient which he has learnt directly or indirectly in his professional capacity as a registered medical practitioner. The death of a patient does not absolve the doctor from this obligation.

There are exceptions to this general rule which may justify disclosure of confidential information:

1. The secrets are those of the patient, hence you are at liberty to disclose them with his or her consent or that of his or her legal adviser.
2. There are legal rules which oblige you to pass on information, for example notification of births and deaths, infectious diseases, poisonings under the Factories Acts. The Abortion Act, Misuse of Drugs Act and Road Traffic Act require the doctor to disclose information under certain circumstances.
3. When your patient is receiving clinical care from colleagues who are bound by, or fully appreciate, your ethical code of secrecy, information necessary for that care may be shared.
4. Information regarding your patient may sometimes be given in confidence to a relative – general practice is conducted on that basis of mutual trust. Be careful, however, if you choose to impart information to others, that you have satisfied yourself of their *bona fides*.
5. General practice is now recognized as a rich source of information for medical research. Projects should be approved by a recognized ethical committee; you should be satisfied that you are content for the information to be divulged and, if in doubt, it is as well to decline agreement pending permission from the patient.
6. If, in the course of legal proceedings, a court requires details of your patient's confidential medical history, that information is not privileged from disclosure but you need a formal sealed court order, or if you are in court the direction of the judge or presiding officer such as the chairperson of a bench of magistrates before you comply. It is sensible to seek advice from your protection society rather than attempt to deal with this matter unaided.
7. A situation may arise when you have the dilemma of deciding whether your duty of confidentiality to your patient is outweighed by your duty to society – if, say, the

patient continues to drive when you know his or her medical condition makes that unlawful, or police are investigating a serious crime and you are asked to divulge information which may assist that investigation. Again, talk this over with a colleague or your society secretariat before acting.

Some of the common questions asked in this context are:

Can I disclose other colleagues' entries? What about the hospital letters? Are the records not the property of the Secretary of State...

The doctor with whom the patient is registered is said to have 'Possession, custody and power' over the records and as such has the responsibility for disclosure delegated to him or her. Look again at what has been requested; if it is the whole record and you are not sure whether you should proceed, seek advice, but the whole record means precisely that, not edited highlights, part pages of the clinical records or the omission of reports or letters. It is a relatively simple matter for a solicitor to acquire a court order for disclosure in appropriate cases and you stand every chance of an order for the costs being made against you. A complete set of photocopies is acceptable for disclosure and you can recover the costs in providing them.

Is the patient's solicitor allowed to have the notes, should it not be another doctor?

The solicitor is allowed to have the notes, to read them and to discuss the content with his or her client — your patient — unless you alert the solicitor to a part of the history which it may be inappropriate to reveal to the patient and the solicitor gives an undertaking that that part of the record will not be disclosed.

It is clear that the notes should consist only of entries which you would be prepared to have read aloud in court. Any alteration to notes should be initialled and, if for whatever reason additional notes are made, the date on which they were written should be clear. Any attempt to tamper with notes after they have been made is a serious matter, the doctor doing so risking action by the FHSA/HB, the GMC or even criminal prosecution.

Medical reports

Requests for 'a report' about a patient are common and may be made by the patient, a solicitor, insurance company, or a colleague acting on behalf of one of these. Sometimes the police ask for a report. Consider the issues of confidentiality as outlined above. The Access to Medical Reports Act 1988 (AMRA) provides an individual patient with the right of access to a report on him or her made for the purpose of employment or insurance by a doctor who has, or has had responsibility for the clinical care of the patient. The common 'Private Medical Attendant's (PMA) form used by insurance companies is an example of a report caught by the provisions of AMRA but there are many others, and consideration should be given as to whether AMRA applies in each case. The Act requires, amongst other things, that the patient be given twenty one days in which to signify a wish to see the report before it is sent off, and to agree to it being sent, having previously been made aware of the right to withhold consent, to see the report and to request amendments before it is sent. The doctor must retain a copy of the report for six months. The patient retains the right of access during this time.

If the report is not for the purpose of insurance or employment, ensure that the patient is aware of the request and has given consent.

It is prudent to preserve a copy of the report and the consent. Reports should be confined to the matter in hand — be cautious if you face an open-ended question or one concerning your patient's lifestyle.

If you harbour any doubts, invite the patient to see you and discuss the issues in question with him. Take advice if necessary.

Negligence

Negligence is a failure to exercise a duty of care, resulting in damage (see also chapter three).

No doctor takes kindly to the proposition that his or her care of a patient has fallen below acceptable standards and if such an allegation is made, perhaps by the patient's solicitor, it may be tempting to make a rapid, angry, ill-considered response. Nothing is gained by doing so, least of all will it persuade a solicitor to withdraw the allegation.

The solicitor's letter is a signal for the doctor to seek the advice of his protection society without delay. It is unwise simply to put the letter to one side or dispose of it in the hope that the whole matter will disappear. It will not. The solicitor's letter, the 'Letter before Action', may give little information about the basis of the case, or make statements which are inaccurate in part, in that the letter represents the patient's point of view.

It is for the doctor, aided by the appropriate protection society, to produce a rebuttal; this requires the close collaboration of all concerned, with the notes being a central piece of evidence.

Once disclosure of the notes has taken place (see above), the patient's advisers will seek their own expert medical opinion and if that is supportive of the patient's case they will issue a writ, followed by the definitive document of their case, the 'Statement of Claim', which will set out who the defendants are and the particulars of the alleged negligence.

Occasionally a solicitor may issue a writ without a prior warning. If a writ is served on you this calls for immediate action, because failure to acknowledge service of the writ within fourteen days automatically risks judgement being entered against you, irrespective of the merits of the case.

It is essential to contact your protection society as soon as you are served with a writ.

The investigation of the claim begins by seeking detailed comments from all involved. Some time may well have passed since the events in question, and as the notes are crucial they may need to be retrieved via the FHSA/HB and perhaps transcribed if the writing is difficult to read!

The member of secretariat will ask various questions to clear up any doubts, and will then seek expert opinion(s) as needed. A meeting of clinicians, experts, solicitor acting for your society and member of secretariat will clarify the issues. Legal counsel advises further, including whether or not the case should be defended to trial or settled out of court.

Few doctors look upon the prospect of appearing in court as the principal witness in defence of their own name with anything other than misgivings. It may be some comfort to know that the majority of claims are discontinued by the plaintiff; of those that go forward the majority are settled out of court on the basis that no liability for negligence is accepted. There remains a small percentage which go to trial − and of these some trials are on the issue of the quantum of damages only (see Figure 5.1).

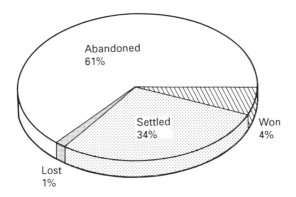

Figure 5.1 Outcome of 500 cases, reported to The Royal Commission of Civil Liability and Compensation for Injuries (The Pearson Commission), published 1978

Advice concerning appearances in court is given in chapter two.

The changing face of practice is likely to include changes in the range of procedures being undertaken in the surgery. This expansion of role brings in its train a need to counsel the patient about the procedure and its consequences, to warn of common sequelae and to obtain specific consent where appropriate.

Complaints to Family Health Services Authorities/Health Boards

The Secretary of State for Health is responsible for the provision of primary care services and discharges this duty ultimately via the Family Health Services Authorities (Health Boards). Each maintains a list of medical practitioners (and others not relevant here) who are in contract with it. The day-by-day activities of the contractors are overseen by the general manager. It is he who receives complaints.

Not all complaints concern matters germain to the doctor's terms of service and the delegated officer will deal with them himself, often without any need to inform the doctor, unless in his view the complaint suggests the need for the doctor to be alerted: repeated complaints about a doctor's 'attitude' or a receptionist's rudeness might be examples of this.

If a complaint is received which, on the face of it, suggests the possibility of a breach of the doctor's terms of service, the officer will discuss the matter(s) with the chairman of a sub-committee of the FHSA/HB known as the Medical Services Committee and various options are then open to the chairman.

The informal procedure (see Figure 5.2)

Some Family Health Services Authorities have begun to use this mechanism only comparatively recently and the procedure

The complaints procedure

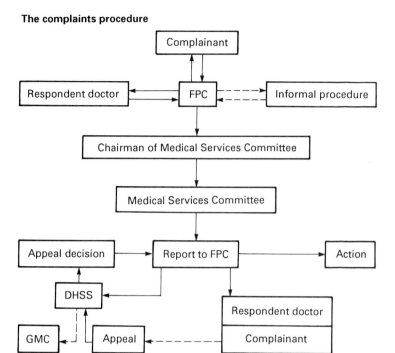

Figure 5.2 The complaints procedure

itself varies. It may be an exchange of correspondence between the parties, the FHSA/HB acting as 'honest broker'; some prefer to arrange a meeting, with a lay person appointed by the FHSA/HB acting as conciliator. The object is to air the complaint, and allow discussion, explanation and reconciliation to take place, without recourse to more formal proceedings. Many complaints are resolved in this way, and the FHSA/HB will seek this solution whenever possible. Neither 'side' gives up the right to ask for the formal procedure to be brought into action at the conclusion of the informal one. If a formal investigation takes place subsequently, none of those considering the complaint, except the chairman, knows what has gone before. A doctor cannot be found to be in breach of his or her terms of service as a result of an informal procedure.

Are there any disadvantages in agreeing?

Sadly, some patients know and 'play' the system, and, by judging the weight of the explanation given to them informally, recognize the weaknesses in their case and have an opportunity of strengthening them before a formal hearing. It must be said that such an attitude is not common, but does exist.

Before describing the formal procedure, a word of explanation of the terms in use may help.

The *complainant* may be the patient(s), relative(s), a friend, or if the patient has died, anybody.

The *respondent* is the doctor; there may be more than one respondent according to circumstances. In general terms the letter of complaint gives the information necessary to identify the doctor(s) but even if the complaint does not name the doctor − 'The doctors at the XYZ Health Centre' − the delegated officer has a duty to discover precisely who is involved.

A *party* to the complaint is a doctor who is involved but who does not have a contract with the investigating FHSA/HB, and who cannot be found to be in breach of any terms of service. A doctor who is considered a party to the complaint is entitled to take a full part in the proceedings and be present throughout, a doubtful privilege some might think!

A *witness* is invited to give his or her account at the relevant moment and is then asked to leave, thus knowing nothing of the proceedings as a whole.

The *Medical Services Committee* (MSC) is a sub-committee of the FHSA/HBC and has the duty of investigating complaints, reaching conclusions based on findings of fact and making recommendations to the FHSA/HB (see below).

The formal procedure (see Figure 5.2)

In contrast with the foregoing, the FHSA/HB must follow the rules set out in the 'Service Committee and Tribunal' Regulations and must consider, firstly, when the complaint was received.

Complaints received outside a specified period (currently thirteen weeks) since the incident, must not be considered automatically. The delegated officer must approach the complainant to enquire the reason for the lateness of the complaint. The reply is seen by the chairman of the service committee who, if satisfied, will invite the full committee to consider the reason for lateness (not the complaint as a whole), and if the committee is satisfied the respondent is notified that a complaint has been received, that it is out of time, that the committee consider the reasons for lateness are reasonable and the respondent doctor's agreement to proceed is sought.

The doctor may find a discussion with a member of secretariat helpful at this stage, perhaps in conjunction with the secretary of the Local Medical Committee (LMC) in order to decide upon the reply and to give appropriate help in its preparation, remembering that the committee seeks comments on the issue of lateness, not on the complaint as such at this point.

If the service committee, or the doctor(s) concerned, withhold agreement to a formal investigation on the grounds that the complaint was submitted out of time and that the reasons for lateness are unacceptable, the complainant has the right of appeal to the Secretary of State and will be given all the necessary information to enable him to exercise that right. It is by no means uncommon for complaints to be allowed to proceed when out of time.

The first hurdle overcome, the delegated officer now seeks the comments of the respondent(s) to the complaint; a period of four weeks is allowed in which to reply.

It is natural for a doctor to feel a sense of outrage when a complaint is received. It may also be understandable for him to dash off a reply in an effort simply to brush the complaint to one side. It would be foolish to do so.

The prudent doctor will re-read the complaint, the letter from the FHSA/HB and the notes, take advice and construct a reply which is accurate in its content, can be corroborated by a combination of notes, letters or reports from hospital and which answers each point made by the complainant, mentioning *en passant* those issues over which there is no dispute.

The letter of response should be typewritten and be professional in its style, bearing in mind that it will be the core of the defence and will be read by the members of the service committee as well as the complainant. Highly technical terms will only serve to confuse the lay people and are best avoided. It is sensible to begin with a word of regret at having received the complaint and then to follow a logical course through the facts of the case, being specific about the time and date of an event, who spoke with whom, who saw the patient and what transpired by way of history, examination, advice, prescription and disposal. The purpose is to demonstrate that the doctor was in a position to make a reasonable judgement of the case at each stage.

The letter may well end with a note of concern or sympathy, and a comment to the effect that the doctor does not believe that he or she is in breach of the terms of service. It may be helpful to include copies of documents which have been referred to in the letter and to discuss the case with the author(s) of letters it is intended to use and to seek their views. The letter of response should not be used as an opportunity to vilify or score points over the complainant, however outrageous the complaint.

The committee will reach the appropriate conclusion by reading the carefully constructed reply. The complaint will come to an end if the complainant is satisfied with the reply or if the MSC is satisfied that there has been no breach of the terms of service. If neither of these applies the complainant is asked for his comments on the letter of response.

The chairman must now decide whether the case should be considered on the basis of the papers submitted or by way of an oral hearing, the latter is more likely if there are fundamental differences revealed in the correspondence. All the papers are sent to the parties and the members of the committee at least three weeks before the hearing. The Medical Services Committee comprises a chairman (who is often legally qualified), and a minimum of two lay members and two general practitioners, the delegated officer or his assistant and a clerk are also present.

Each 'side' can be assisted, provided that the 'friend' is not a solicitor or barrister for if he is, he is not allowed to address the committee or to question any witness. A representative of the local Community Health Council will often act as complainant's friend; the secretary of the appropriate Local Medical Committee and the protection society secretariat have wide experience of committee procedures, and will advise the doctor who would be most appropriate in the particular circumstances of the case. Colleagues who are experienced in acting as doctor's friend are in heavy demand, and early notification of the date of any hearing is essential.

Irrespective of who goes to the hearing as respondent's friend, do remember that service committees prefer to listen to what is said from the doctor's own lips rather than hearing it from a third party.

The conduct of a hearing

The hearing is not a court of law, strict rules of evidence do not apply. The chairman will begin by introducing all concerned, then dealing with the question of paid advocacy. The complainant is asked if he has anything he wishes to add to what is in the papers before the committee; many do so, often to the detriment of their case. The committee now question the complainant, then the respondent doctor or his 'friend' (see above) can do the same. It is perfectly possible to plan the questions to put to the complainant in order to make the weaknesses in his case clear. Beware of asking questions which occur to you on the spur of the moment — they have a habit of backfiring!

The complainant may now call and question his witness(es), the committee asks questions, then the respondent. Only ask questions which have some point, again these can be planned in advance, but be careful not to repeat a question already asked by someone else. Speak to the complainant in a normal tone of voice which betrays nothing of any inner feelings!

The complainant's case is now completed and the same order of presentation is open to the respondent. A carefully written letter of response will be in the papers already supplied to the committee, who will be familiar with it and any supporting documents. Further statements at this stage often serve no purpose, thus unless the complainant has raised an issue which merits immediate comment, it may be best to add nothing at that stage and the committee will then pass straight on to their questions, followed by those of the complainant and/or friend. Once more, it may well be possible to predict many of the questions, and it is here that time spent in preparation, using a colleague as 'devil's advocate' shows its value. Some questioning may be abrasive or apparently biased, but unless the chairman disallows a question, answer it in a calm clear manner. The golden rule is never to lose your composure, you are the professional and your demeanour will be a point in your favour, especially if it contrasts sharply with that of the complainant.

Any witness(es) are now called. The case will have been discussed in depth with each one. The questions to be put (and the answers) will have been discussed, so there should be no surprises now! Keep the questions brief, to the point and strictly within the sphere of knowledge of the witness, avoiding hearsay. When you have finished with each witness, the committee and then the complainant have their turn and the witness is asked to leave. Do not be tempted to bring more witnesses than are of positive use, the committee will not be swayed by weight of numbers.

Finally each side can summarize and the respondent has the advantage of going last. Complainants often repeat all that has gone before and weary the committee; be careful to avoid that pitfall. If the case has gone as planned, it may well be best to say that there is nothing to be added to the facts which the committee have before them, and it remains to thank the committee for their attention.

This is the end of the hearing and the parties are asked to leave. The committee now deliberates, in private, to reach its 'findings of fact', to draw conclusions from them and thence to make recommendations to the FHSA/HB.

The sequelae to a hearing

The FHSA/HB consider the recommendations of the Medical Service Committee and almost invariably endorses them. The parties are then notified of the result, which will be either that the complaint is *dismissed*, or that the complaint is *upheld*.

The respondent doctor is then subject to one or more of a variety of options from the FHSA/HB:

1. A warning to comply more closely with the terms of service.
2. A withholding from remuneration, the sum being commensurate with the 'offence' and any previous adverse findings on record.
3. An application to the NHS Tribunal that the doctor's continued inclusion in the Medical List is prejudicial to the efficiency of the NHS General Medical Services.
4. The imposition of a limit on the doctor's list size.
5. The respondent doctor may be obliged to reimburse any out-of-pocket expense the complainant has incurred as a result of the doctor's breach of the terms of service.

Financial penalties are considered as civil debts.

The papers from a Service Committee are forwarded to the Department of Health, and the Secretary of State may refer the case to the GMC.

Either party can appeal an adverse decision, but the complainant cannot appeal in order to increase the penalty. Most careful consideration should be given to the question of whether to appeal, for it is within the power of the Secretary of State to increase the penalty; thus a case which may not have been referred to the GMC as a result of the first investigation, may be the result of an appeal. 'Bruised ego' is not sufficient grounds for appeal!

As an alternative to an appeal, representations can be made to the Secretary of State against the amount of the withholding as a single issue, the advantage being that if the decision of the FHSA/HB is upheld the doctor does not run the risk of the withholding being increased. There is often a delay of about four weeks between the hearing and the MSC recommendations being considered by the FHSA/HB, approved and notified to the parties. A period of four weeks is allowed in which to lodge notice of appeal.

If an appeal is made by either the complainant or respondent, the Secretary of State can be asked to order a re-hearing of the case or to consider the matter on the papers alone. If, for whatever reason, the doctor has not taken advice up to this point, now is the time to do so; the conduct of an appeal is a highly skilled matter, beginning with the letter of appeal itself.

An appeal by way of re-hearing is conducted by a tribunal comprising a chairman who is legally qualified assisted by two general practitioners. The evidence is heard on oath. Legal representation is allowed. The case follows the pattern of procedure described above, but it is open to either side to call new witnesses or introduce such evidence as is seen fit.

The tribunal considers the case and reports to the Secretary of State. The findings are made known to the parties concerned, often many months later.

Records, prescriptions and certification

Records

Medical students are taught to make systematic notes according to a set formula, with the intention of initiating a lifelong habit. All too often these skills learned on the 'nursery slopes' become eroded with the passage and pressure of time. Good notes are medicolegal armour, as well as a requirement of the terms of service of an NHS general practitioner.

Clinical notes serve the writer and others concerned with continuity of care. Should there be an allegation of want of care, perhaps via a complaint or a civil action in negligence, then well-written, legible and dated notes, which demonstrate an orderly approach to the case, would render the defence of the action much easier. Notes must not be altered in the face of criticism; to do so is not only foolish, but puts the doctor at risk of criminal prosecution or referral to the GMC.

If additions are made, they should be clearly dated to show when they were written. The notes are likely to be an important piece of evidence before the court; clinical records are no place for wit, sarcasm or invective – which is more likely to make the writer appear foolish than to impress.

How long should records be preserved?
How much can I prune notes?

The safe answer is to keep everything, for the very entry, letter, laboratory or X-ray report which is discarded could be the one to unlock a difficult medicolegal conundrum and save the doctor much anguish. Perhaps a reasonable compromise would be to cull correspondence which duplicates information.

The increasing use of computers in general practice will inevitably mean more clinical notes being stored electronically. Computers have a finite capacity, thus some system for saving memory space will be necessary. The importance of ensuring that contemporaneous records are preserved (perhaps using hard copy) and that the records themselves are tamper-proof, such as to satisfy the courts, are problems for the software manufacturers.

Orderly record keeping in general practice comprises more than clinical notes. It is sensible to formulate a practice policy dealing with the method of receiving messages, recording them in a systematic fashion, whether at home or at the surgery, to show the time the message was received, what was said and by whom, what action was planned and took place, and what disposal occurred. Ancillary staff operating such a system are more likely to feel secure while the doctor, on-call at home, is less likely to forget to hand a patient back to a colleague in an orderly fashion. A book laid out with space for the information is not easy to ignore!

General practitioners receive large quantities of post daily, much of which prompts further action. A method by which the staff know that post has been seen and read, by all concerned, and that appropriate instructions have been given will minimize the risk of reports being filed away prematurely. Several civil claims arise each year as a result of failure of communication.

Prescriptions

General practitioners write thousands of prescriptions annually. The format of a prescription is governed by Act of Parliament — for example it must provide the name and address of prescriber and patient (and age of the latter if under 12), be written in indelible ink, be dated and signed by the prescriber.

Under the terms of service, the NHS prescription may not be endorsed to include a repeat dispensing of the items. The doctor must use the form provided by the FHSA/HB for a prescription, on which is printed the doctor's identification number with the FHSA/HB, useful for a number of purposes including PACT (an analysis of the doctor's prescribing pattern compared with his local and national colleagues), and for payment of doctors who have dispensing practices.

Prescription forms are provided in large numbers by the FHSA/HB. The doctor must ensure security for the bulk item and also for the pad in current use.

Doctors' writing is traditionally the butt of humour. If prescriptions are written illegibly and the wrong drug dispensed, the consequences for both doctor and patient are serious.

Certification

A medical certificate, report or notification required by law may only be issued by a registered medical practitioner. There are many instances when the doctor is asked to confirm the accuracy or truth of a statement or document, and this carries both privilege and a heavy burden of responsibility. A doctor's signature on a document is accepted without question; should it be shown that the doctor has acted carelessly or been guilty of dishonesty he can expect a heavy penalty. The General Medical Council's 'Blue Book' sets out guidance for practitioners, and false certification will be likely to lead to an allegation of serious professional misconduct (see below).

The wise doctor will be sure that the facts are correct, and refer to a known patient, before agreeing to sign his name. On no account should a doctor issue a certificate entitling the patient to sickness benefit unless he has seen the patient for himself, nor should he sign a form, such as a passport application form, unless the criteria laid down can be satisfied.

The General Medical Council

The GMC is a governing body for the profession, first established by the Medical Act 1858 in order to enable members of the public to distinguish qualified and unqualified practitioners. The purpose of the Council was to establish and maintain a medical register, to supervise the content and standard of medical education and to act as a disciplinary body. While a number of subsequent Acts of Parliament have altered the details, including the provision of the Health Committee, the basis of the Council's duties remains unchanged as a self-regulatory body within the profession.

The Council publishes a pamphlet 'Professional Conduct and Discipline: Fitness to Practise' containing current guidance. New editions are issued from time to time.

Complaints to the GMC may come from various sources:

1. The courts, following conviction of a criminal or common law offence in the British Isles.
2. The Department of Health, following a complaint to an FHSA (see above).
3. A professional colleague.
4. A patient, relative of a patient, or a member of the public who has sworn an affidavit in support of his or her complaint.

If the 'Preliminary Screener' of complaints is satisfied there is a *prima facie* case to answer, the doctor is invited to submit a written explanation, after taking suitable advice, for consideration by the 'Preliminary Proceedings Committee' (PPC). This committee may take no action, write to the doctor with cautionary advice, or refer the case on to the Professional Conduct Committee (or Health Committee).

Common reasons for an appearance before the Professional Conduct Committee (PCC) are:

1. Conviction for a criminal offence in the United Kingdom especially an offence involving dishonesty such as theft, false certification, fraud or forgery, drink-driving offences, assault, and offences involving illegal abortion.
2. Irregular professional relationship with a patient, a breach of professional trust including obtaining loans or gifts from a patient and improper disclosure of information.
3. Improper behaviour, usually of a sexual nature.
4. Failure to provide a reasonable standard of care.
5. Abuse of professional privilege, such as issuing a false or misleading certificate. The council has regarded the prescription of drugs of dependence, other than in the course of *bona fide* treatment, as serious professional misconduct.
6. Ethical matters such as disparagement of a colleague.
7. Canvassing or advertising. Information for patients must not be substituted by self-promotion. The doctor must be able to justify his actions should it be said that he was attempting to gain a professional advantage over a colleague.

The procedure of the PCC is similar to a court of law. The doctor will be legally represented if he wishes, evidence is heard on oath and witnesses can be subpoena'd to attend. The PCC can postpone a decision on a case, dismiss it, or it can find against the doctor and admonish him, impose conditions on his registration, suspend his registration or direct that the doctor's name be erased from the Register. The last three options are subject to a right of appeal to the Judicial Committee of the Privy Council.

6 General surgery

N. C. Keddie

Delays in diagnosis
  Acute abdomen
  Malignant disease
Complications of investigations
  Upper gastrointestinal endoscopy
  Colonoscopy
  Laparoscopy
  Biopsy material
  Vascular investigations
Operative complications
  General
  Head and neck surgery
  Gastrointestinal surgery
  Groin surgery
  Varicose vein surgery
Postoperative complications

General surgeons are not considered to be a high risk for medical negligence claims, but they have been affected by the overall increase in the number of claims in recent years. The scope of general surgery is still very wide but many so-called general surgeons now confine their work to a single body system – vascular, gastroenterology with its subdivisions, endocrinology – yet in the emergency situation and isolated district hospitals, the general surgeon is expected to be competent and experienced in many fields. When things go wrong and the patient sues, experts acting for the patient are often surgeons who have special experience of the condition concerned, and state that only surgeons with such experience should be dealing with it. The courts, naturally, place great store on the opinion of such experts. Despite such circumstances, this chapter will cover the field which conventionally is called general surgery.

The problem will be approached by considering delays in diagnosis, complications of investigations, operative complications and failures in communication (including informed consent). Sadly, the last is a common source of claims in all fields of medical negligence.

Delays in diagnosis

Two common areas where problems arise are the acute abdomen and malignant disease.

Acute abdomen

Acute appendicitis

This is a common source of problems, especially in young children when symptoms may be atypical. When diarrhoea is present, this can easily mislead the unwary clinician. Patients, not unnaturally, expect a common disorder to be diagnosed promptly and treated successfully. Thus, claims are very common when complications arise. The most serious complication is death for which claims are common, but residual abscesses and obstruction due to adhesions complicating late appendicitis are also a source of claims. Recently there have been a number of claims for infertility due to pelvic adhesions coming many years after the complicated appendicitis.

Ectopic pregnancy

This is another potential disaster area and frequently is seen initially by a general surgeon. The menstrual history is often unhelpful, especially in women with irregular periods, and pregnancy tests on the urine may be negative. It is a diagnosis which must be considered in females of reproductive age, as the symptoms are frequently atypical. The consequences of a delayed diagnosis can be disastrous if the patient suffers torrential intra-abdominal bleeding when the warning symptoms are ignored.

Acute intestinal obstruction

Increasing numbers of claims are appearing for delays in this diagnosis. It is usually claimed that the delay resulted in bowel resection which could have been avoided by earlier diagnosis. The symptoms are frequently atypical, misleading the clinician and leading to understandable delay. Provided care has been taken and full notes made, claims can be confidently defended. The history of previous surgery should raise the suspicion of acute adhesive obstruction. A small femoral hernia in the obese patient is another common trap. In the latter situation, the bowel may be incompletely obstructed causing further confusion as the patient may have diarrhoea and not the expected absolute constipation.

Torsion of the testis

Still too frequent a cause for claims is this missed diagnosis.

Young patients with acute scrotal swelling are given antibiotics for 'acute epididymo-orchitis' when they should be submitted to urgent exploration of the testis. This can rarely be defended.

Abdominal trauma

This can cause considerable difficulty in diagnosis. Penetrating injuries are notorious traps for the surgeon. Careful, clear observations with full records are essential if mistakes are to be avoided. Patients with visceral or vascular trauma can be misleadingly well on arrival at hospital, causing a false sense of security. Surgeons must be suspicious in cases of abdominal trauma to avoid missing the diagnosis.

Malignant disease

Breast carcinoma

A constant source of claims is the missed breast carcinoma. This may result from reassurance being given to a patient with an ill-defined breast mass without biopsy or mammography. Biopsy can be so readily performed with either fine needle aspiration or a trucut needle. A more recent problem is the false negative mammogram, the patient presenting with a clinically obvious malignant mass within a short time. The public must be carefully educated about the limitations of breast screening, particularly regarding false positive and false negative results. Claims are now arising where a mastectomy has been performed from mammographic evidence of carcinoma, not confirmed on histology. Clearly, biopsy is essential in these cases to confirm or refute the radiological findings.

Gastrointestinal carcinoma

Claims for delayed diagnosis of gastrointestinal carcinoma are very common. Patients with dyspeptic symptoms are given hydrogen blockers for prolonged periods without investigation. The trap here is that these drugs can relieve the symptoms of gastric carcinoma, and even allow malignant ulcers to heal. It is acceptable to treat a patient on first attendance with hydrogen blockers, but in the 'at risk' age group they must be followed up and investigated if they do not respond promptly.

Large bowel carcinoma is very common, and its incidence is increasing, but still patients are told their rectal bleeding is due to piles without being properly examined or investigated, sometimes delaying the diagnosis for many months. In other cases, a barium enema has given a false negative result and it is the radiologist who is subjected to a claim.

Skin tumours

Skin tumours are notoriously difficult to diagnose clinically, and malignant melanoma gives rise to considerable problems. Where a long waiting list exists for minor operations, patients thought to have a benign lesion can linger, awaiting operation while the disease progresses and, understandably, they sue when it is discovered that their lesion is malignant. The amelanotic melanoma is a notorious pitfall. Squamous carcinoma is not always obvious in its features. The only message is that when any doubt exists about a lesion, urgent excision must be arranged.

Complications of investigations

Increasingly complex technology has provided powerful tools for improving diagnostic accuracy but 'invasive' investigations have inevitable complications in a small number of patients. It is here that informed consent is so very important when planning such investigations.

Fibreoptic endoscopy is now very widely available and many thousands of these procedures are performed each year. A small complication rate is inevitable, and has been carefully documented by detailed multi-centre studies conducted by the British Society for Digestive Endoscopy. When patients sue for complications of these procedures, provided the procedure has been performed properly by experienced practitioners and the complication is promptly recognized and treated, a confident defence can be mounted.

The vexed topic of informed consent inevitably arises in this context. Is it the doctor's duty to forewarn each patient of all the possible complications of the procedure? In general in the United Kingdom, if the chance of the complication is very low, it is not considered to be good practice to burden the patient with the anxiety of the remote possibility of a rare complication. On the other hand, certain specific complications need to be mentioned so that the patient has the option of refusing the investigation. Opinions in this area vary and are changing, the danger being that, with increasing litigation, there will be a gradual move over to the attitude prevalent in the United States of America where, every complication is mentioned in detail before any procedure is performed.

Upper gastrointestinal endoscopy

Perforation

This is a common cause for claims. The pharynx may be damaged when there is difficulty introducing the instrument. When strictures of the oesophagus are present, benign or malignant, damage may occur during attempted introduction of the endoscope or if dilatation is attempted. After dilatation of oesophageal strictures, a wise precaution is to avoid oral fluids for at least six hours and to perform a chest radiograph looking for gas in the mediastinum.

Perforation is a well-documented complication of endoscopy. If it arises in the hands of an experienced operator, and is promptly recognized and treated, a successful defence can be mounted.

Aspiration pneumonia

The sedatives used for endoscopy suppress the cough reflex so it is possible for secretions to be aspirated into the branches of the bronchial tree. If this is not recognized, a lung abscess may follow.

Endoscopic retrograde cholangiopancreatography

Acute pancreatitis can occur even during diagnostic ERCP and warning should certainly be given about this. It can be fatal. A successful defence is possible if a claim is made, provided the procedure was properly performed and the complication recognized quickly and properly managed.

Colonoscopy

Perforation

This can occur as a result of instrumentation by inexpert operators. The end of the instrument may tear the wall of the colon. The other possibility is that the colon may be split when a loop is formed by the instrument if the operator continues to push it in when the tip of the instrument will not advance. If operative procedures are performed through the colonoscope, for example polypectomy or biopsy, there is an increased risk of perforation. Late perforations may occur through a diathermy site following polypectomy.

The rigid sigmoidoscope continues to be a common source of claims and the Medical Defence Union was recently unsuccessful in defending an experienced surgeon who caused this complication, promptly recognized and successfully treated it. This ruling went against the general view that this is a recognized complication which has happened in the hands of many experienced operators. Biopsy through the rigid sigmoidoscope is notorious for producing perforations. The difficulty in defence occurs when it is not recognized until peritonitis develops and the patient is desperately ill.

Laparoscopy

General surgeons are taking much more interest in this procedure now in the wake of the gynaecologists. The Royal College of Obstetricians and Gynaecologists have carried out an excellent survey of complications of the procedure by obtaining detailed information from their Fellows. General surgeons have been sued for causing bowel damage, bile leakage and haemorrhage as a result of performing operative procedures through the laparoscope or by causing damage during its introduction. Defence is possible if an experienced operator is involved and the complications have been managed properly.

Biopsy material

Claims are increasing for errors involving biopsies. The amount of tissue obtained through flexible endoscopes and laparoscopes is small. The 'wrong' piece of tissue may be obtained to provide a correct diagnosis, or interpretation of the appearances may be difficult. The message is that several biopsies need to be taken at any one time, and repeat biopsies done if clinical doubt exists; for example about an oesophageal stricture or gastric ulcer. Another source of disaster is the labelling and handling of biopsy specimens. When a long list of endoscopies is performed and several patients have biopsies taken, it is all too easy for errors to arise. Errors can occur in the endoscopy suite or during the histological processing. If the histology is not in keeping with the endoscopy findings repeat biopsy may be needed if an unnecessary resection is to be avoided. Such claims are usually indefensible.

Vascular investigations

Arteriography

These may be performed by the radiologist or clinician and

may be combined with therapeutic procedures, such as an intraluminal angioplasty in arteriosclerotic stenoses. Haematoma at the site of arterial puncture can occur or damage to the artery used for access causing ischaemia in its distribution. Thrombosis of the vessel under investigation or peripheral embolism from the site of the lesion are a frequent source of claims. The most expensive claims involve the cerebral circulation where permanent brain damage may occur. Should warnings of these possible complications be given? The medicolegal climate now prevailing would lead to an answer in the affirmative, but there is some interesting evidence to suggest that fear of the complications may increase their incidence so it is a controversial problem.

Operative complications

Space allows only a few common problems to be mentioned. The question of surgical responsibility constantly arises when claims are made. It is always difficult to define the degree of experience required before allowing a surgeon to perform certain procedures without supervision, and a frequent source of claims relates to the question of delegation of surgical operations to surgeons in training. Another potential source of danger is when lists are carried out at two separate sites nominally under the control of one consultant surgeon, who clearly cannot be in the two places at the one time. When problems arise with his junior colleague it may not be possible for him to go rapidly to his aid if he is working in another hospital, sometimes a considerable distance away. It is critically important for consultants to make their employing authority aware of the potential risks of such arrangements, although, since the introduction of Crown Indemnity in the UK, the cost of any settlement will be borne by the authority.

In the National Health Service demands on consultants' time sometimes result in them leaving junior surgeons with work that they should not be doing. There is no defence when claims follow from this. The Confidential Enquiry into Perioperative Deaths published in 1987 by the Association of Surgeons and the Association of Anaesthetists (see p. 158), has brought to light deficiencies in senior cover, particularly for emergency work. Another common arrangement which gives rise to the problems is where a junior surgeon works in a twin theatre with his chief 'next door'. The consultant is thus close by if his junior colleague needs help or advice. The reason this is a common source of claims is that the young surgeon has done the damage which gives rise to the claim before realizing that he needs help from his senior colleague. It takes considerable experience to realize when you need more senior help while performing an operation.

Consider now some of the more common sources of claims following on operative procedures:

General

Minor operations

These are often done by inexperienced surgeons, and, since the recent publication of a Government White Paper, by general practitioners, in less than ideal circumstances.

Superficial nerve injury is the most serious complication, frequently causing claims. The spinal accessory nerve is very vulnerable during lymph node biopsy in the posterior triangle of the neck.

The vulnerable position of the lateral popliteal nerve makes it a common source of difficulty. It can be ligated during varicose vein surgery. In addition, extravasation of sclerosants used to inject veins in the vicinity of the nerve can cause damage. It can also be injured by tight bandaging following surgery or injection treatment of varicose veins.

Superficial lumps on the course of nerves must be treated with great circumspection. A schwannoma will usually separate from the nerve but often the nerve is damaged by inexperienced surgeons before the nature of the lesion is appreciated.

Bad scars

These frequently cause claims so it behoves all surgeons to learn about skin creases. The deltoid and presternal areas are notorious for producing keloid scars.

Wrong operations, and retained swabs and instruments

These problems continue to be reported to the Medical Defence Union despite the detailed checking system now in use. Human error cannot be completely eliminated, but it cannot be stressed too strongly that the recommended procedures, jointly agreed between the Royal College of Nursing and the defence organizations, must be adhered to rigidly if these infrequent but nevertheless indefensible errors are to be eliminated.

Head and neck surgery

Recurrent laryngeal nerve injuries

These injuries during thyroidectomy continue to cause claims. If the nerve has been exposed clearly, and the surgeon is experienced in thyroid work, defence is possible. If both recurrent laryngeal nerves are damaged defence is not usually possible. It is advisable to warn patients of possible voice changes after thyroidectomy. The external laryngeal nerve is perhaps at greater risk than the recurrent laryngeal nerve during thyroid surgery, but so far no claims have been made for injury to this nerve.

Facial nerve injuries

These injuries following parotid surgery are difficult to defend and preoperative warning of this possibility is essential. It is accepted that special interest and experience in parotid surgery is advisable for a surgeon considering this type of operation. It is not an area into which the occasional surgeon should venture. This question of increasing specialization within general surgery is causing increasing difficulty in successfully defending the so-called general surgeon, who clearly cannot be widely practised in every procedure that could come under the heading of general surgery.

Gastrointestinal surgery

Common bile duct injuries

These injuries, which occur during cholecystectomy, continue to be commonly reported to the Medical Defence Union and can very rarely be defended. There is an increasing tendency now only to use operative cholangiography selectively, where specific indications exist for the presence of stones in the common bile duct. This is clearly acceptable for very experienced biliary surgeons, but the operative cholangiogram is a valuable means of demonstrating the anatomy of the biliary tree very clearly, and thus cutting down the risk of any damage to the biliary duct system. There is still a case for carrying out an operative cholangiogram on a routine basis for this reason, rather than for seeking unsuspected common bile duct stones.

Impotence following rectal surgery

Claims for this problem raise the question of whether warnings about this possibility should be given preoperatively. It seems very cruel to warn a desperately ill young man needing urgent surgery for ulcerative colitis that he may become impotent following surgery. Sadly, if he does, he is likely to sue when he is fully recovered from an otherwise successful operation. The claim can be defended on the basis that it is a recognized complication, but an expert proctological opinion may state that it is preventable as the *nervi irrigentes* should be protected during mobilization of the rectum. In malignant disease claims can be defended in that a more extensive operation is needed to cure the disease.

Injection treatment of haemorrhoids

This has produced a large number of claims due to the sclerosant being injected into the capsule of the prostate. This can result in severe haematuria, prostatitis or retention of urine.

Groin surgery

Inguinal hernia repair

This is obviously performed many hundreds of times each year and frequently by the less experienced surgeon who considers hernia repair to be a valuable training ground. Claims for wound sinuses (related to the non-absorbable suture material used for the repair) are common and can be successfully defended. Testicular atrophy is another common problem and provided the procedure has been properly performed by an experienced surgeon, this can be defended on the grounds that it is a well described and documented complication.

Vasectomy

Sterilization procedures have led to a plethora of claims. As vasectomy is performed for a patient's benefit and not, as is usual in surgery, because of some disease, it is crucial that all possible complications of the procedure are explained to the patient so that he is aware of these prior to making the decision about whether or not to go ahead with the procedure. The patient must be warned that it is extremely difficult to reverse the procedure, and that the success rate of doing so is probably around 50%. In addition, he must also be warned that there is a failure rate, although this is very low (about one in ten thousand). Warnings concerning the need for postoperative sperm counts are absolutely essential, and full records must be made that these warnings have been issued to the patient. In addition to this it is probably wise to mention that scrotal haematoma, infection and even, very rarely, testicular atrophy, are possible problems that can arise. All these have led to claims. The need for two postoperative sperm counts, a week apart, at about twelve weeks following the operation, must be fully explained. Histology on the vasa is advisable.

Any procedure which is done for social convenience or cosmesis rather than to deal with pathology is likely to be followed by a claim if complications arise. Careful records are thus absolutely essential. It is not adequate several years later, when the claim for recanalization arises, to say that your normal practice is to warn patients of this risk. There has to be written evidence that a warning was given, and it is now advisable to include it in the consent form signed by the patient. It is a common problem for the Medical Defence Union to be unable to defend their member simply because he or she has kept inadequate records. This is very frustrating when there is no evidence of negligence in the way the surgery was performed.

Varicose vein surgery

Femoral vein damage

Femoral vein damage remains a frequent source of problems. This occurs during mobilization of the long saphenous vein prior to ligating it. The bleeding can be torrential but is easily controlled by a pack until senior help can be obtained. A small tear at the sapheno-femoral junction can be carefully repaired with a vascular suture. If a segment of femoral vein is badly damaged the gap needs to be bridged. A cylinder of suitable length and diameter can be fashioned from saphenous vein. Artificial graft materials are not satisfactory in the long term.

Lateral popliteal nerve injury

Each year several cases are reported to the Medical Defence

Union of ligation of lateral popliteal nerve in mistake for a vein in the vicinity of the neck of the fibula. These claims clearly have to be settled.

Injection treatment

Injection treatment of varicose veins has already been referred to in the context of nerve injury but commonly extravasation of sclerosant produces tissue damage, either leading to unsightly pigmentation or complete full thickness damage to the skin and subcutaneous tissues causing ulceration. This may well have to be excised and grafted leaving unsightly scars about which the patient, understandably, makes a claim. Even more serious is when the sclerosant is injected in error into the posterior tibial artery when injecting veins on the medial side of the ankle. This produces ischaemic damage of variable extent in the forefoot.

Postoperative complications

All text books on operative surgery devote a considerable amount of space to postoperative complications, and all experienced surgeons are well aware of such complications and have had to deal with them. Despite this, they are increasingly considered to be a justifiable reason to sue the surgeon. Patients are now expecting perfection from surgery. This is especially true where the only indication for the operation is cosmesis, for example in the field of plastic surgery, or commonly with varicose veins. It is absolutely essential to warn patients of all the possible complications when this type of procedure is performed. Wound infection, stitch sinus, postoperative adhesive obstruction, post-appendicectomy intra-abdominal abscess and testicular atrophy following hernia repair are all recent examples of claims. Deep vein thrombosis and pulmonary embolism are common causes of claims if no prophylactic measures have been taken, or the patient was on the pill.

Usually, defence is possible and an expert opinion leads to the claim being dropped. On the other hand, if basic steps in preoperative care are not clearly recorded, for example, prophylactic antibiotics in appendicectomy, defence can be very difficult.

Communication with patients and their relatives is obviously an essential part of the practice of good medicine. It is also vital in reducing the risk of negligence claims. This is especially true when surgery 'goes wrong'. If frank explanations are provided, most patients accept the situation with good grace. Communication between colleagues is also just as important, for example, when the care of a patient is handed over, at weekends or holiday periods. Cases of undiagnosed abdominal pain must be reviewed by the duty surgeons and patients with postoperative problems must be fully discussed, so that their care is not neglected when the surgeon primarily responsible for their care is absent. Claims frequently arise when communication of this kind between colleagues has been inadequate, and such claims are entirely avoidable.

7 Obstetrics and gynaecology

E. M. Symonds

There are no official figures published of the number of claims against obstetricians in the United Kingdom, but unofficial estimates suggest that over the last five years there has been a threefold increase in claims in obstetrics and gynaecology. This rate follows the overall pattern of increase, but the claims contain a disproportionate number of potentially large settlements because of infants with birth-related injuries. The maximum awards have risen from £132 970 in 1977 to £1.03 million in 1987, (see Kings Fund Report 1988) and it is these settlements that have largely been responsible for the steep rise in subscriptions to the Medical Defence Organizations.

Obstetric claims

Birth-related injuries

Obstetricians have for some years now found themselves locked into a situation that, when being associated with a difficult or traumatic delivery, or with the management of acute fetal distress that is associated with the birth of a child with a cerebral abnormality, brings the risk of a negligence claim.

In North America, this has resulted in a crisis in maternity services in some states where the combination of a contingency fee system for lawyers and abnormally high settlements for pain and suffering have made it impossible to provide insurance at a realistic level. In two states, namely Florida and Virginia, this resulted in the introduction of legislation for no-fault compensation for birth-related injuries. In the United Kingdom it is now 15 years since the first major claim appeared in the case of *Whitehouse* v. *Jordan*. By 1988, it has been estimated that some 300 new claims were appearing each year. This rate may not be sustained because it represents 'historical' recruitment dating back 21 years. Nevertheless, if only one birth in 5000 results in a cerebrally abnormal infant, this could account for a minimum of 120 new claims each year.

Cerebral injury may result as a consequence of direct trauma or in association with birth asphyxia or a combination of both problems.

Traumatic delivery

Relatively few claims arise on the basis of trauma to the fetus, and, with the awareness of the threat of litigation, most obstetricians now avoid difficult instrumental deliveries and resort increasingly to Caesarean section.

In the case of *Whitehouse* v. *Jordan*, an allegation was made that the obstetrician pulled 'too long and too hard' on the forceps in attempting to deliver a child from a woman of short stature with a small pelvis. This child was delivered by Caesarean section but subsequently exhibited microcephaly and mental retardation. The original judgement in favour of the plaintiff was successfully appealed in both the Appeal Court and the House of Lords, and some ten years after the first hearing, Jordan's name was cleared of the allegation of negligent practice.

Essentially, Lord Denning made it clear at that time that provided a clinician acted with reasonable clinical skill and care, he should not be held responsible every time there was an adverse outcome. The difficulty lies in deciding what constitutes reasonable skill and care. Every 'trial of forceps' puts that judgement to the test and in many centres this has now led to the abandonment of mid-cavity forceps delivery. Obstetricians are now well advised to think carefully before becoming involved in difficult vaginal deliveries, and should not perform difficult rotations and excessive traction if they are to avoid the risk of litigation.

Occasional claims arise as a result of trauma from forceps blades to the eyes or face, or because of fractures sustained during difficult deliveries such as those associated with impacted shoulders.

Birth asphyxia

The majority of obstetric claims now arise as the result of

allegations of negligent management of cases where the child is born asphyxiated and subsequently suffers from cerebral palsy and mental retardation.

The claims largely centre on the interpretation of cardiotocograms (CTGs), which provide a continuous analogue recording of heart rate and intrauterine pressure.

This may apply to both antepartum and intrapartum recordings. All practising obstetricians know the limitations of antenatal cardiotocographs. Even assuming that the interpretation of heart rate patterns is consistent from one clinician to another, it is well known that an abnormal tracing one day may be followed by a normal tracing the same day. A decision therefore has to be made on a composite of factors such as the gestational age, evidence of intrauterine growth retardation (IUGR), other complicating maternal conditions and other methods of assessing placental failure.

No one test can be considered in isolation to constitute an immediate cause for action.

Recent studies with fetal blood samples by cordocentesis (Soothill et al., 1987) have shown that chronic hypoxia and acidosis can be demonstrated in 30% of babies diagnosed as suffering from intrauterine growth retardation. Such infants may exhibit abnormal CTGs but the extent of asphyxial cerebral damage the child may have suffered in utero before a decision is made to deliver it will always be uncertain, even if the initial diagnosis of asphyxia is made with certainty by direct acid-base measurement on cordocentesis.

Claims relating to intrapartum management generally allege that in the presence of evidence of fetal distress, no action was taken or that action was taken too late or that the heart rate recording was technically unsatisfactory or something should have been done about it. If a specific decision is made to avoid electronic fetal monitoring, unless this is by specific instruction from the mother, then an abnormal outcome is likely to be followed by litigation.

Cardiotocography is high on sensitivity and low on specificity. It is good in diagnosing what is normal and substantially over-diagnoses abnormality. This is particularly true in the second stage of labour where gross variations in heart rate occur in up to 40% of women, and most of these infants are healthy at birth. These arguments have recently been discussed in a review by Jenkins (1989). The subject is further complicated by the fact that many infants born with abnormal CTGs and clear evidence of severe acidosis at birth, as judged by cord blood measurements, show no evidence of any ill effects.

Conversely, infants born with normal cord blood pH and a low Apgar score may subsequently show significant abnormalities.

These are complex problems and do not lend themselves easily to arguments in a court room. They are, however, common problems in perinatal management and the present implications are that where a child is born that has cerebral damage, the person who has attended the birth process is liable to be subjected to litigation. There are substantial problems in assessing the significance of abnormal cardiotocographs because these lie at the heart of most claims concerning management. If one can assume that certain patterns of heart-rate change are abnormal, then the issue arises as to how often and for how long an abnormality must persist before it is considered negligent not to intervene. In a court room, it is likely that expert witnesses may, with complete integrity, give directly conflicting views about the interpretation of the same heartrate record.

Avoidance of litigation in perinatology

Many cases of litigation where perinatal brain damage has occurred follow a common pattern, and whilst it is not possible for anyone involved in perinatal care to avoid legal action:

1. When using antenatal cardiotocographs, make sure that they are seen and signed by an informed member of the medical staff. Where a recording is abnormal, a specific decision should be recorded even if this is simply to state that no further action is required *pro tempore*.

2. Intrapartum cardiotocographs are a constant source of difficulty. Make certain that the technical quality of the recording is adequate to enable interpretation. If it is not satisfactory, then the monitor or the scalp electrode lead or the abdominal transducer should be changed. It is better to manage a labour with intermittent auscultation rather than unsatisfactory electronic fetal monitoring.
3. CTGs should be annotated on a time and event basis and all records should be retained.
4. Care must be taken with the transfer of information at the changeover of staff so that continuity of care is maintained.
5. A clear policy on management should be defined so that there are guidelines for action to be taken when an abnormal CTG occurs.
6. There is no point in recording the heartrate unless some notice is taken of the result. The application of a monitor does not in itself confer any advantage on the patient unless the information it provides is used appropriately.

Multiple pregnancy

Several claims have now arisen relating to the management of the second twin. All data recorded in the literature indicate that there is a significantly higher mortality and morbidity rate in second twins. This is related to intrapartum asphyxia associated with placental separation or cord prolapse and with traumatic delivery of the second twin.

The legal process once again highlights what can be considered to be reasonable obstetrical practice. How long, for example, is it reasonable to allow between the delivery of the twins? What presentations are acceptable as being safe to anticipate vaginal delivery? There are no precise answers to these questions and all that can be said, with certainty, is that if the clinician wishes to avoid the risk of litigation arising from intrapartum management, then all multiple pregnancies should be delivered by elective Caesarean section. Already there is an increasing tendency to deliver the second twin by Caesarean section where there is an abnormality of presentation. Junior staff no longer have the confidence or experience to perform manoeuvres such as internal version and breech extraction, and therefore tend to resort to second twin section. This is not without its risks, both to the mother and the fetus, as the additional delay involved in effecting delivery where a fetus is already asphyxiated may be more hazardous than performing an immediate breech extraction.

The ruptured uterus

Most problems with uterine rupture occur through a previous Caesarean section scar. Partial or complete extrusion of the fetus into the peritoneal cavity follows, leading to fetal death or damage. Most claims are based on the assertion that the rupture should have been anticipated or that too great a time elapsed between the time of rupture and the time of surgery. Where hysterectomy is necessary, a claim often follows that relates to the loss of reproductive function. Such claims often arouse great bitterness amongst the doctors concerned with the management, who find themselves facing allegations of negligence where they may have spent many hours and exercised considerable skill in keeping the patient alive.

The statement of claim commonly includes reference to the presence of pain preceding the rupture. In reality, very few cases of uterine rupture are preceded by any warning signals, whereas lower abdominal pain rarely indicates uterine scar dehiscence.

The only safe way to avoid claims relating to Caesarean section scar rupture is to perform a repeat elective section in all cases where there has been a previous Caesarean section.

Bladder and ureteric injuries

Claims relating to bladder damage, ureteric injury and consequent fistula formation are relatively uncommon in relation to pregnancy. The problems often occur where the bladder has been adherent to the lower segment from previous surgery or where there is extension of a lower segment incision laterally, with haemorrhage from the uterine vessels. Attempts to control this haemorrhage may then result in damage to, or suture enclosure of, the ureter. It may be difficult to defend injury to the bladder at Caesarean section if the procedure is uncomplicated, whereas damage to a bladder that is abnormally adherent to the lower uterine segment may be an acceptable complication. Damage to both ureters at the same operation will rarely be accepted as defensible.

Prenatal diagnosis

Techniques of prenatal diagnosis of congenital abnormalities have become increasingly sophisticated, but medicolegal problems, have been incurred in their wake.

These difficulties have related to:

1. The failure to offer appropriate advice concerning prenatal diagnosis where it is necessary so that the opportunity to have the pregnancy terminated is lost.
2. Failure to advise the patient of the risk of the technique.
3. Failure of the diagnosis because of tissue culture failure necessitating a further amniocentesis and cell culture.

With the expansion of clinical genetic centres and increasing sophistication in both diagnosis and therapy, claims in this specialty are likely to increase.

Already, claims are arising from the failure to identify specific abnormalities by ultrasound screening, even though the resolution and quality of ultrasound imaging continues to improve. Lack of experience in the ultrasonographer would not be considered a reasonable basis for resisting a claim relating to a missed diagnosis when more expert advice may be available.

Gynaecological claims

Complications of sterilization

Overwhelmingly the commonest reason for gynaecological litigation is failed sterilization. These claims follow a pattern with one of two assertions:

1. That the procedure was incorrectly performed.
2. That the patient did not give informed consent and claims that had she known of the risk of failure, she would not have consented to the operation.

Until about 1980, it was not common practice to notify the woman of the risk of failure on the grounds that this was a rare event, and that informing the patient that there was a risk of failure simply led to confusion and unnecessary anxiety.

Nowadays, it is routine to warn the patient of both the risk and incidence of failure.

The situation should not lead to 'punitive' sterilization where hysterectomy or bilateral salpingectomy may be performed to make absolutely sure that no failure will occur. Some women do change their minds and reversal of clip sterilization carries a substantial chance of success. The author has never seen, in 15 years of advising about the risks of failure, any woman change her mind and not proceed with the operation because there was a risk of failure.

Should both partners by involved in the counselling?

In the recent case of *Gold* v. *the Haringey Health Authority*, the plaintiff complained that the procedure of sterilization was incorrectly performed because she conceived again, and that she was not advised of the risk of failure. She alleged that had she known this information she would have persuaded her husband to have had a vasectomy. She claimed support for the unwanted child but then knowingly went ahead and had a further pregnancy.

The argument on causation, namely that recanalization of one or both tubes had occurred, was accepted in court and as the woman had a subsequent hysterectomy, the specimen was available showing both clips in the correct place on both tubes.

The judge found for the plaintiff on the consent issue not because the method failed, but on the basis that the husband should also have been counselled about male sterilization. This decision was subsequently overturned in the Appeal Court.

It should, however, be clear that the failure to apply clips to the correct structure is not defensible. In these circumstances, pregnancy usually occurs within three or four months of the sterilization procedures. Some recent claims have arisen as a result of ectopic pregnancies following sterilization and in particular, allegations that the patient was not informed about the possibility of tubal pregnancy. In practice, very few clinicians would offer such advice on the basis that it is unnecessarily alarming to instruct the patient about the relatively low risk of ectopic pregnancy. Sterilization, for example, has a high risk of failure if performed at the time of delivery or after a termination of pregnancy because of the oedematous and vascular nature of the tubes. Provided the woman is advised of this risk, then it is not negligent to sterilize a patient at this time because there are circumstances where it may be particularly important to perform a sterilization at the time that the woman is available or where the tubes are 'available' when the woman is delivered by Caesarean section.

Complications of abortion

Claims arising in relation to abortion are common, and principally arise from two complications:

1. Trauma to the pelvic organs.
2. Failure to terminate the pregnancy.

Trauma to the pelvic organs

Traumatic injuries generally occur as a result of perforation of the uterus during cervical dilatation or during the removal of the conceptus, either by suction evacuation or by the use of sponge holding forceps. Perforation often results in subsequent damage to bowel and omentum and it may also result in haemorrhage from the perforation site either into the peritoneal cavity or into the broad ligament. Perforation is a recognized and accepted risk of pregnancy termination, and in itself does not constitute negligent practice. It is the management of the complications arising from perforation that most commonly result in litigation. Long delays in recognizing bowel perforation and the development of peritonitis are difficult to defend, and where there is any question of bowel perforation, a laparotomy or laparoscopy should be performed.

Failure to terminate the pregnancy

Termination failures most frequently occur when the pregnancy is early, and when the small early embryonic sac is missed. The commonest explanation submitted by the medical staff is that the uterus must be bicornuate and that only one horn was evacuated. This is rarely the correct explanation.

There is no failsafe way of avoiding this problem, excepting to ensure that all women undergoing termination of pregnancy are requested to return for a follow-up visit six weeks post-operatively, and are examined vaginally to ensure that the pregnancy has been terminated. It is widely recognized that many women do not keep these follow-up appointments either with the hospital or the general practitioner but if they are given that opportunity, the case may be easier to defend.

Some court actions have been brought as a result of ongoing pregnancies which were present before a period was missed and were present at the time of sterilization. This is defensible, provided the patient was not actually overdue with her period at the time of the procedure. It is, therefore, particularly important when patients are booked in for sterilization that the date of the last menstrual period is determined, and the operation is either deferred or precautions taken to ensure that pregnancy has not occurred before the sterilization is performed.

Complications of hysterectomy

Damage to the bladder and to ureters is an accepted and well recognized complication of hysterectomy, particularly where the operation is difficult as the result of malignant or inflammatory disease or in the presence of endometriosis. Nevertheless, the development of a fistula following either a vaginal or abdominal hysterectomy, even where a subsequent primary procedure cures the problem, is often followed by a claim of negligence.

To some degree, common sense dictates what is defensible and what is indefensible. For example, ligation of both ureters in the performance of a routine hysterectomy performed by an inexperienced and inadequately supervised trainee surgeon would not be considered defensible, whereas damage to one ureter by an experienced surgeon during a difficult hysterectomy with extensive endometriotic scar tissue in the pelvis would certainly be defensible.

Prompt recognition of damage to the bladder or ureters always enhances the prospect of defending a case. All training hospitals face the difficulty of deciding when a staff member is adequately trained and experienced to undertake procedures unsupervised. If restrictions on what is considered to be suitable are too severe, the risks to patients are simply transferred to a later date.

Intrauterine contraceptive devices (IUCDs)

Product liability has effectively removed intrauterine contraceptive devices from the market in the USA and may well have the same effect in the United Kingdom. Claims rarely arise on the basis that the device failed and that pregnancy occurred with the device 'in situ' because it is widely recognized that, as with barrier methods, there is an acceptable failure rate. However, legal claims often arise from insertion procedures that result in uterine perforation or where the vaginal threads are lost and no specific action is taken to ensure that there is a device still in the uterine cavity.

IUCDs or displaced tubal clips that lie free in the peritoneal cavity rarely cause any problems because of involvement with the bowel or bladder. A claim is only therefore likely to arise if there are specific symptoms associated with the displaced device.

Swabs and packs

All surgeons know the importance of swab counts and nursing checks at the end of any operation. It is the responsibility of both the nursing staff and the surgeon to ensure that no swabs or packs are left in the abdominal cavity or vagina unless by design for specific reasons.

In reality, the commonest mistake is to leave a pack or swab in the vagina after suturing an episiotomy. The reasons for this mistake are that the surgeon is often unattended, that no swab counts are made either before or after suturing is complete, and because there is often considerable bleeding from the perineal wound and from the uterus which obscures the retention of a swab.

Any accidentally retained pack or swab is effectively indefensible, and it is therefore essential that swab counts should be correct and that a vaginal examination should be immediately performed at the completion of episiotomy repair to ensure that all swabs are recovered before the mother leaves the labour ward.

Conclusions and recommendations

1. Obstetricians around the world know that they are being sued at an increasing rate and for rapidly increasing sums of money. The sums of money involved are a threat to the continuation of obstetric and midwifery care.

2. Good case records are essential if there is to be a reasonable chance of defending a case. This means that records must be kept on file for at least twenty-one years.

3. Claims arising from intrapartum management often relate to poor signal/noise ratios so that spurious and misleading records are made. It is pointless to continue with an unsatisfactory recording, and the clip or machine should be changed.

4. Abnormal fetal heart rate patterns demand a response. That response may be to continue with the labour unless the heart rate deteriorates or it may be to deliver the child. It is not acceptable to attach a monitor and then to ignore the record when it is unsatisfactory.

5. Failed sterilization is the commonest reason for litigation in gynaecological practice. It is defensible provided the patient has been adequately counselled and provided the initial procedure was correctly performed.

6. Delegation of procedures must be made only where the level of experience of the trainee is adequate.

7. Good note-keeping generally helps in the defence of a claim. Poor note-keeping is never of assistance to the defendant.

References

Jenkins, H. M. (1989) Thirty years of electronic intrapartum FHR monitoring – Discussion paper. *Journal of Royal Society of Medicine*, **82**, April, SM – 214

King's Fund Institute (1988) *Medical Negligence – Compensation and Accountability*, (eds C. Ham, R. Dingwall, P. Fenn and D. Harris), Briefing Paper **6**, KFI, London

Soothill, P. W., Nicolaides, K. H. & Campbell, S. (1987) Prenatal asphyxia, hyperlacticaemia and erythroblastosis in growth retarded fetuses. *British Medical Journal*, **294** No. 6579, 1051 – 1053

Whitehouse v. *Jordan* (1981): 1 WLR 247

8 Orthopaedics

T. E. Jeffreys

Allegations
  Battery
  Breach of contract
  Negligence
Missed or delayed diagnosis
Consent to treatment
Negligence in treatment
  Retained instruments
  Splintage
  Tourniquets
Conclusion

Orthopaedic surgeons are among the high risk groups identified by the defence organizations of the United Kingdom and the Republic of Ireland; although, by all accounts, they are not yet as at much risk as their peers in the United States. Until January 1990 they paid for this privilege with higher defence subscriptions than their colleagues in more sluggish branches of medicine. This financial burden has been eased by the introduction of Crown Indemnity, but the risk of being sued remains unchanged and there are fears that the introduction of Crown Indemnity will result in a tendency to settle actions at the expense of vigorous defence of the surgeon's good name.

Allegations

Many allegations of negligence are, in effect, complaints of misinformation, or lack of information. Many British surgeons do not talk enough to their patients. Nowadays, patients feel they have the right to full discussion of their problems, and the right to participate fully in decisions concerning their management. Many actions would not have begun if open and honest exchanges of views had taken place between surgeons and their patients or their families. Any consultant surgeon must be freely available to talk with his patients and their relatives. Patients understand that surgeons can make mistakes without being negligent. However difficult if may be for a surgeon to admit error, such a frank admission may well abort any further action.

Some allegations are mischievous and their receipt is wounding. They can best be countered by a prompt disclosure of medical records. Good notes are the essential defence in all accusations of negligence. Orthopaedic surgeons are better placed than most in this regard, thanks to their long established custom of keeping typewritten clinical records. Even so, the quality of notes overall is lamentable; as anyone knows who has tried to carry out a retrospective clinical review.

There are three allegations that patients can make against doctors in British law.

1. Battery.
2. Breach of contract.
3. Negligence.

Battery

This is the touching of a person without his or her consent. Such consent is tacitly understood to have been given when a patient is examined during consultation. It is wise to have a nurse present when a female patient is examined. Women of some ethnic minorities object to discarding their clothes for examination. An orthopaedic examination, of the spine for instance, is inadequate unless the patient is fully undressed. Diagnoses can be missed if this elementary rule is not followed. Patients who refuse to undress for examination should be told that the surgeon cannot accept responsibility for errors of diagnosis or management which may result from unobserved physical signs. They must sign a form of absolution for such responsibility.

Breach of contract

It would be an unwise surgeon who promised a certain outcome to any particular treatment. This applies with particular force to orthopaedic surgery which attempts to repair, reconstruct or replace damaged tissue. When a procedure is being explained to a patient it is convenient to use mechanistic phrases and diagrams, but the patient must understand that his body is not a washing machine or a motor car, and that no guarantees can be given.

Negligence

Every surgeon has made, or will make, an error of judgement. Such errors are not negligent, provided they are made in good faith and for positive reasons, after analysis of a problem and after consideration of alternatives. Some errors are the result of carelessness and are indefensible, in conscience or in law. Amputation of the wrong limb or digit because of incorrect preoperative marking is an extreme example, but the wrong operation can be performed if strict theatre discipline is not maintained. No matter how detailed a protocol for avoiding errors is adopted by any hospital, it remains the individual surgeon's responsibility to ensure that he is carrying out the right operation on the right patient.

Negligence may also be alleged if the patient has not been warned of any possible risks associated with any particular procedure, operation or drug prescription. The patient may also allege negligence if he consents to a certain advised form of treatment, when alternative forms of treatment were not explained and offered to him. A patient dissatisfied after a Keller's operation for *hallus valgus*, for example, may allege that the surgeon was negligent in not explaining, and offering, the alternative procedure of metatarsophalangeal arthrodesis, or *vice versa*.

Negligence may be alleged after missed or delayed diagnosis, after treatment, and after the outcome.

Missed or delayed diagnosis

When a patient with multiple injuries is first seen, the most life threatening lesion demands immediate attention. If a thorough examination is not carried out then, less obvious injuries may not be detected, only to become apparent later with embarrassing consequences. Patients unconscious from head injuries provide the clearest example, when spinal injuries and fractures of the peripheral skeleton may escape detection. Suspicion must be high, until eliminated by complete clinical, and if necessary, radiographic examination. Every unconscious patient with a head injury, for example, must be assumed to have a fracture of the cervical spine until there is radiographic confirmation of the contrary. In an ideal future world, total body-scanning of every casualty will eliminate error. It will also eliminate the need for clinical acumen in casualty doctors. But until that happy day, complete, well-recorded clinical examination is still the best defence against the missed diagnosis.

Radiographs are essential, but they must be used to support and confirm clinical suspicion, not to replace it. Too often, the clinical examination is cursory and the wrong part X-rayed. Well known traps, such as the misinterpretation of referred pain, can lead to errors of diagnosis which are indefensible. Patients with injuries to the hip may present with knee pain, the knee is examined, and X-rayed, but the hip is not and the fracture or dislocation is missed. Patients with severe injuries to the knee, or a fracture of the femur, must be examined and X-rayed to exclude hip injury. Omission to do so is indefensible negligence.

Even worse is to rely on radiographs alone, without examining the patient. Fractures are frequently complicated by injuries to other structures, to nerves, blood vessels, ligaments and tendons. The consequences of these associated injuries may well be more serious than the fracture itself, and failure to detect them is inexcusable.

If clinical suspicion leads to a request for radiography it is essential that those radiographs are adequate. If a neck injury is suspected and an X-ray of the cervical spine is requested, that radiograph must demonstrate the whole cervical spine. Fractures of the sixth and seventh cervical vertebrae are missed because the films do not extend below the level of the fifth vertebra. It is often difficult for the radiographer to demonstrate the lower cervical spine because the patient has a thick neck or bulky shoulders. Such inadequate films must not be accepted. There are various radiographic techniques available to demonstrate the whole cervical spine, and the clinician must not be satisfied until these have been exhausted. If adequate films are still not available then the opinion must be so qualified. To write 'cervical spine NBI' (no bony injury) when one has not seen the whole cervical spine is to court disaster.

The other notorious example of a clinical opinion expressed on inadequate radiographic evidence is the fractured carpal scaphoid. It is now accepted that failure to obtain special views of the carpal scaphoid is negligent. It is standard teaching that the radiographs should be repeated after a two week interval, in order to exclude a fractured scaphoid absolutely, but this dictum has recently been challenged; and it has also been suggested that isotopic scanning is a cheaper and equally reliable substitute (King and Turnbull, 1981; Leslie and Dickson, 1981; Dias *et al.*, 1990). Such arguments are fiercely contended amongst hand surgeons. The vulnerable casualty officer is advised to stick to the old teaching.

Some orthopaedic conditions, other than injury, are uncommon and the junior doctor, or the general practitioner may have little experience of them. In part, this is due to the scanty exposure undergraduates have to orthopaedic problems, but ignorance of a condition does not excuse failure to elicit physical signs. The limping child is the flagrant example. An unexplained limp in a child or an adolescent must be explained. Pain from a hip lesion is referred to the knee and a cursory examination of a normal knee in a child with Perthes' disease or an adolescent with a slipped upper femoral epiphysis will not do.

Examples of missed diagnoses abound, but principles always apply. A thorough inquiry of history, a complete physical examination, accurate recording of findings — including negative findings, and a willingness to seek advice from other colleagues, will protect against later allegations of negligence. The law does not demand omniscience from doctors, merely that they act as competently as is in accordance with their level of education, training and experience.

Consent to treatment

A patient consenting to treatment must understand to what he is giving consent. He must understand not only what is proposed in the treatment but what the objectives are, and what the risks of that treatment are. The surgeon may be accused of negligence if he does not disclose those risks. He is, however, allowed to use his medical judgement whether he should disclose all risks involved in a course of treatment. The principle was put to the test in the House of Lords in the case of *Sidaway* v. *Bethlem Royal Hospital Governors and others* in 1985. In that case the plaintiff sustained permanent neuro-logical disability after an operation performed for the relief of cervical discogenic pain. The case for the plaintiff was that she would not have consented to the operation if the risk of such neurological damage – estimated as being of the order of 1% to 2% – had been conveyed to her before the operation. The claim was dismissed at appeal because the Law Lords held that the surgeon had acted in accordance with a practice rightly accepted as proper by a body of skilled and experienced medical men (see Legal Correspondent, 1984). There are certain situations where informed consent is difficult or impossible to obtain. The patient may be so severely injured as to be incapable of informed consent. Consent should then be sought from the nearest relative, but if none is available the surgeon must exercise his clinical judgement and carry out whatever treatment, in his opinion, is in the patient's best interests (see Medical Defence Union, 1968).

Parents have a special responsibility when giving consent for operations on their children, and it is essential that they clearly understand the possibility of complications that may occur. When matters do go wrong in operations on children, parental grief is compounded by an inevitable sence of guilt which they will tend to project in accusations of neglect by the surgeon. In orthopaedic surgery this has particular poignancy when con-genital deformities are corrected operatively. The parents already feel guilty in being unwittingly responsible for the deformity, and if the disability is increased after the operation their added guilt will manifest as anger and a demand for retribution. Operations on the spine for scoliosis carry a risk of inflicting a neurological defect, even paraplegia. The parents must be made aware of this risk. The British Scoliosis Society has paid attention to this by issuing an advisory pamphlet for such parents. This form of consent should be used in addition to the more general consent to an operation (see British Scoliosis Society, 1988). It can be argued that by overemphasizing these risks, parents will be discouraged from allowing correction of deformity at an early stage, with the consequence of the deformity increasing to a point where any corrective procedure is more difficult, and carries an even greater risk of neurological damage. This may well be so, and is a sad example of the influence of 'defensive' medicine on sound surgical practice.

Negligence in treatment

Every patient is entitled to expect that his treatment is carried out with competence. In orthopaedic surgery, treatment includes 'closed' manipulations as well as 'open' operations. Technical advances in orthopaedic surgery have transformed the results of the treatment of injuries, and of 'cold' orthopaedic conditions. Patients' expectations have also been transformed and imperfect results are too often attributed to negligence. As surgical operations have become more sophisticated, so their complications have become more frequent and more significant. Total replacement of major weight-bearing joints has transformed the lives of sufferers from chronic arthritis, but the incidence of deep vein thrombosis following such operations is disturbingly high. Prophylaxis against venous thrombosis carries the risk of postoperative haematoma formation with consequent problems of wound healing, infection and possible failure of the implant. Some orthopaedic surgeons object to prophylactic anticoagulation for those reasons and also because the value of such prophylaxis is not absolutely established. Is the failure to institute prophylactic anticoagulation in high risk patients negligent?

Some errors in operations, such as amputation of the wrong

limb, are criminally negligent and cannot be defended. Others may result from the distortion of expected anatomy or unexpected pathology. In this category fall such mishaps as the inadvertent division of nerves or crucial blood vessels. Such events must be clearly recorded, in full detail in the operation note. They are, however, difficult to defend.

Peripheral nerves are often damaged in surgical operations. Lesions can be produced in many ways; by cutting, by traction, by tourniquet pressure or direct pressure on an unprotected part in an anaesthetized patient. Sometimes the nerve injury is difficult, if not impossible to avoid. Open menisectomy incisions can divide cutaneous nerves, leaving persistent areas of numbness or paraesthesia. Digital nerves may be so intimately involved in Dupuytren's fascia as to be at significant risk during fasciectomy.

Injury to a major nerve during an operation is difficult to defend. Awareness of the risks, a thorough knowledge of anatomy, and a meticulous operative technique are the best safeguards (see Bonney, 1986).

Retained instruments

Instruments and swabs continue to be left in wounds with dismal frequency, as perusal of the annual reports of the defence societies shows. The surgeon must take precautions against this. These precautions consist of allowing time for the swab and instrument count to be completed, and acknowledging that the count has been completed satisfactorily. Rigid theatre discipline is necessary, using the procedures standardized for any particular hospital. The relevant safeguards are laid out in the 'Joint Memorandum' issued by the Medical Defence Union and the Royal College of Nursing. It is sad to observe that despite the publicity given to this most notorious of surgical errors, the incidence of retained foreign bodies has fallen hardly at all (see Medical Defence Union and Royal College of Nursing Memorandum, 1978).

Splintage

After orthopaedic operations on limbs, either open or manipulative procedures, the part is often splinted in a plaster of Paris cast. Swelling of the limb under such a splint can obliterate the circulation, causing pressure sores, muscle necrosis, nerve lesions or even gangrene of the limb. Whenever possible the cast should not be circumferential. This can be achieved by applying a plaster slab in the first instance, or by splitting the complete cast after it has been applied. Tight bandages, or compressed wool can be equally dangerous. Constant vigilance must be maintained on the distal extremities. Any alteration of sensation, or colour change in the exposed part must be an indication for immediate release of the constriction. It is not enough to split a plaster cast; the underlying wool must be divided down to the skin and the constriction released until the circulation has returned to normal.

Vascular compression can occur in the unsplinted injured limb from the accumulation of blood or oedema fluid in closed fascial compartments. When this occurs in association with a fracture, it must be remembered that the position of the fracture is of secondary importance to the viability of the limb. If simple measures of repositioning do not result in prompt resolution of signs, the fascial compartment must be quickly decompressed by open operation.

A postoperative X-ray must be taken after any operation involving the division of bone or the insertion of an implant. This X-ray should be done as soon as possible after operation, ideally before the patient has left the theatre suite, so that any correction can be carried out then.

Tourniquets

Many orthopaedic operations are carried out in the bloodless field of an exanguinated limb, occluded by a pneumatic tourniquet. The Esmarch's or Samway's tourniquets must never be used. Pneumatic tourniquets, properly used, are safe provided certain safety rules are followed. The occlusive pressures should be related to the patient's blood pressure. In the lower limb the upper pressure limit should be twice the systolic blood pressure as read in the arm. The upper pressure limit in the arm should be 50 mm of mercury above the systolic pressure (see Klenerman and Hulands, 1979). The duration of applications has been given a reasonable upper time limit of three hours (see Klenerman *et al.*, 1980), although a more recent paper has reiterated the old advice to release the tourniquet after one and a half hours, for five to ten minutes of 'flushing out', before re-applying for a further hour-and-a-half (Sapega *et al.*, 1985).

All tourniquets produce nerve lesions if inflated above the systolic pressure for fifteen or twenty minutes. The numbness and paraesthesia which follow quickly disappear when the pressure is released; but prolonged application can cause more severe damage. In the upper limb the radial nerve is the most vulnerable, but the median and ulnar nerves are also at risk. The risk is small, one in eight thousand cases (Middleton and Varian, 1974), but real enough to make scrupulous attention to detail imperative. Adequate padding must be provided, the tourniquet must be carefully positioned and the pressure constantly checked. Some advise that the gauge be checked before each operation (Flatt, 1972), or that a rocker valve be positioned between the gauge and the cuff (Wheeler and Lipscomb, 1964). It has been shown that an extra wide cuff can be used safely at pressures well below those regarded acceptable with the standard tourniquet (Newman and Muirhead, 1986).

Tourniquet paralysis nearly always recovers spontaneously, but recovery may take three to four months, and the patient may experience distressing causalgia symptoms.

Responsibility for the tourniquet belongs with the surgeon and cannot be delegated.

Conclusion

Orthopaedic surgery has become complex to a degree unimaginable thirty years ago. It also produces complications to a similar degree. Patients have become conditioned to expect brilliant results. Residual disability, no matter how inevitable, is becoming unacceptable to today's patient. When a patient enters hospital with one impairment but leaves with another one he is less likely to accept his lot, and demands to know the reason. If an adequate reason is not given, negligence will be assumed and the surgeon will be blamed. The phrase beloved of lawyers is, *Res ipsi loquitor* — the matter speaks for itself — and it is up to the surgeon to furnish a satisfactory explanation. Unfortunately this leads us to regard all new patients as potential litigants. This attitude damages the relationship between the surgeon and his patients. Its consequences for the progress of surgery will be disastrous.

References

Bonney, G. (1986) Iatrogenic injuries of nerves. *Journal of Bone & Joint Surgery*, **68B**, 9–13

British Scoliosis Society (1988) *Advice for those consenting to spinal deformity surgery*, Pamphlet, London

Dias, J. J., Thompson, J., Barton, N. J. and Gregg, P. J. (1990) Suspected scaphoid fractures. *Journal of Bone & Joint Surgery*, **72B**, 98–101

Flatt, A. E. (1972) Tourniquet time in hand surgery. *Archives of Surgery*, **104**, 190–192

King, J. B. and Turnbull, T. J. (1981) An early method of confirming scaphoid fractures. *Journal of Bone & Joint Surgery*, **63B**, 287–288

Klenerman, L. and Hulands, G. H. (1979) Tourniquet pressures for the lower limb. *Journal of Bone & Joint Surgery*, **61B**, 124

Klenerman, L., Biswas, M., Hulands, G. H. and Rhodes, A. M. (1980) Systemic and local effects of the application of a tourniquet. *Journal of Bone & Joint Surgery*, **62B**, 385–388

Legal Correspondent (1984) Consent to treatment: the medical standard reaffirmed. *British Medical Journal*, **288**, 802–803

Leslie, J. J. and Dickson, R. A. (1981) The fractured carpal scaphoid. *Journal of Bone & Joint Surgery*, **63B**, 225–230

Medical Defence Union (1968) *Consent to Treatment*, MDU, London

Medical Defence Union and Royal College of Nursing (1978) *Safeguards against failure to remove swabs and instruments from patients*, Joint Memorandum, MDU/RCN, London

Middleton, R. W. D. and Varian, J. P. (1974) Tourniquet paralysis. *Australian and New Zealand Journal of Surgery*, **44**, 124–128

Newman, R. J. and Muirhead, A. (1986) A safe and effective low pressure tourniquet. *Journal of Bone & Joint Surgery*, **68B**, 625–628

Sapega, A. A., Heppenstall, R. B., Chance, B., *et al.* (1985) Optimizing tourniquet application and release times in extremity surgery. *Journal of Bone & Joint Surgery*, **67**, 303–314

Wheeler, D. K. and Lipscomb P. R. (1964) A safety device for a pneumatic tourniquet. *Journal of Bone & Joint Surgery*, **46A**, 870

9 Plastic and reconstructive surgery

M. J. Earley

Plastic and reconstructive surgery is a broad based specialty spanning across many disciplines. It has enjoyed several rapid recent advances which have been of advantage to both patients and the specialty itself. These have resulted in a high media profile which finds ready demand for information on replantation of severed parts, treatment of burns and accident victims, correction of gross congenital defects, and an endless thirst for magazine coverage of all aspects of cosmetic surgery.

Several medicolegal problems have arisen as a direct result of the above. New techniques must be mastered with inevitable learning curves, new information must be assimilated by the surgeon and dispensed to the patient, and possible but uncertain complications must be considered. Plastic surgery must always contend with the fact that many results are immediately seen and are readily apparent to the patient. The popular misconception that there are no scars after plastic surgery is all too familiar to those who operate in this field.

In a climate of increasing litigation, the surgeon is more frequently asked to comment on scars, facial and hand injuries, nerve and tendon damage, etc., from both cosmetic and functional viewpoints. Detailed reports and court appearances are becoming more common and the need to remain an 'expert' witness is essential.

One area which has become more difficult in recent years is that relating to cosmetic surgery. It must be stated that there is no such subspecialty as 'cosmetic surgery'. It is a branch of plastic and reconstructive surgery and as such is practised by plastic, not cosmetic surgeons. Advertising clinics encourage the public to believe that a plastic surgeon is not as well versed in facelifts, blepharoplasties, rhinoplasties, etc., and this has resulted in misinformation which the surgeon must correct in order to gain the confidence of the patient. The surgeon must avoid association with advertising and must accept referrals from other medical practitioners only. Self referral is to be discouraged.

Trauma

Where possible, photographs should be taken of the initial injury. Careful examination of the complete patient is essential, and the specialist must not concentrate on that which relates to his specialty alone.

Facial injuries

The first examination of the patient is all important, and if necessary, may have to be carried out under a general anaesthetic. X-rays of facial bones are often less useful than eliciting diplopia from inferior rectus tethering in an orbital blowout fracture, or upper dental arch mobility in a *Le Fort* maxillary fracture. Nasal bone X-rays are notoriously unhelpful as treatment is directed towards correction of external deformity, not towards fixation of multiple bony fragments. If the fracture is undisplaced treatment is usually unnecessary.

The orbital area is often one where difficulties arise. Corneal abrasions and foreign bodies are all too often missed. When possible, specialist ophthalmological opinion should be sought or at least fluorescein used in the casualty department. Canthal drift, ectropion, and webbing of the skin at either canthus can result from missed canthal disruption, a failure to appreciate tissue loss, or poor suturing of the eyelids.

Dirt engraining of facial scars, or indeed of scars of any part are entirely avoidable. All fresh wounds must be adequately debrided either by scalpel or scrubbing brush. Excision of ragged lacerations often results in a better cosmetic result. Careful marking of landmarks will achieve skin cover in many instances where the initial impression suggests loss of skin. Where skin is missing, a primary reconstruction either by flaps or grafts will often give the best result.

Finally, injuries of the facial nerve must always be identified and treated at the first repair. Even the more distal injuries of the nerve branches respond better to a neural microscopic suturing than to a spontaneous recovery. Certainly divisions of the trunk or its main branches must be repaired without delay.

Hand injuries

These have been dealt with elsewhere. A thorough examination based on a sound anatomical knowledge must be carried out. X-rays to rule out foreign bodies or missed fractures are essential. Primary treatment within the first twenty-four hours of tendon and nerve injuries and provision of adequate skin cover must be achieved. There should be close follow-up and supervision, with physiotherapists and occupational therapists playing a role.

Replantation

Patients' expectations must not exceed surgical ability. The patient must be adequately counselled regarding the advisability or otherwise of replantation. Results of single digit replacement are often disappointing and may result in a hand which is more crippled than one where a finger is missing. The surgeon is warned against accepting potential major replants referred by telephone from an inexperienced practitioner, as a patient who has suffered an amputation of an upper limb or leg may also have multiple internal injuries requiring more urgent treatment before transfer to the replant unit.

Skin loss

This merits a separate comment. The apparent rather than real loss of skin in facial injuries has been mentioned. In the limbs, the opposite is often the case. In any crush or shearing injury a degloving of skin from its underlying blood supply must be suspected. The use of fluorescein and ultraviolet light to delineate viability has been well described, but if unavailable, an alternative is cutting back tissue until bleeding is encountered. 'Second look' surgery is also commended, where the limb is re-examined twenty-four to forty-eight hours after the primary surgery, and a further debridement carried out before grafting. The simple pretibial laceration in the elderly is often best excised and grafted in order to avoid prolonged dressings and slow healing.

Unfortunately these injuries are often mismanaged, and referral to a competent practitioner often delayed. Close liaison with orthopaedic colleagues is essential, to share responsibility and to provide rapid and efficient treatment.

Burns

The limitations of burns management outside a burns unit must be recognized. There is no place for the occasional operator, as specialist treatment, both medical and nursing, is desirable. Where possible there should be a designated 'burns consultant' in a plastic surgical centre, who, with an anaesthetics colleague, takes on responsibility for the management of burns, shock, and inhalation burn victims. In this way, mismanagement is avoided. Patients must be aware that the treatment plan is prolonged, and often staged with long intervals between each stage. The long-term complications relating to facial and breast growth in particular should be anticipated, and the possible need for limb contracture releases at a later stage should be appreciated.

Major reconstruction

This section is concerned with the management of:

1. Congenital reconstruction and
2. Post traumatic and post cancer resection reconstruction

Congenital

Cleft surgery

In this type of surgery expectations may often exceed possibilities of treatment. Parents must be aware of the 'average' result, and the practitioner must guard against the temptation of showing his best results in photographic form as a typical outcome. The need for minor revisions of the skin, vermillion and muscle union must be accepted as normal practice and not considered exceptional. The possibility of nasal surgery for alar slump, bone grafting of the cleft alveolus, prolonged ortho-dontic treatment, closure of palatal fistulae, pharyngoplasty for velopharyngeal incompetence and facial osteotomies must be considered and discussed. Support and sensitive counselling in the early stages are essential.

Craniofacial surgery

This has presented to the reconstructive surgeon, with the ability to perform complex procedures, risks ranging from death or blindness, to infection with loss of bone grafts and the need for repeated operations. Again, the provision of infor-mation is all important. Criticism may be levelled at the occasional operator in this field as it has often been demon-strated that complications increase with lack of experience. Team work is essential, and the plastic surgeon must work closely with a neurosurgeon, an oral surgeon, an ear, nose, and throat surgeon, and many others, to obtain acceptable results.

Congenital hand deformities

These must also be treated with compassion, with function being the foremost goal. The patient and parents must be well informed and should not be given false hopes. The surgeon must treat the patient, not the isolated problem, and a result that is a 'triumph of technique over common sense' must be avoided. At all times it must be stressed that appearance is not more important than function. As in other areas, the surgeon must always be prepared to seek expert advice without reluctance or loss of face.

In all of the above areas good record keeping is essential and diagrams and photographs are advisable.

Post traumatic and post cancer resection

Major reconstruction in this field has become a subspecialty of plastic surgery. Informed consent becomes difficult, as many of the techniques are complex, both to explain and fully predict their outcome. The surgeon must be guided by sound ethical principles, while making the patient aware of the advantages and disadvantages of the procedure. Above all, patients must be sufficiently informed to refuse the treatment if that is their choice. One must avoid the temptation to use the latest reconstruction presented at a meeting or published in a journal, because it would be a challenge to try it. There must be good reason behind the choice of reconstruction.

The obsession with one stage surgery is to be avoided, and the patient must not be misled into believing that multiple adjustments of a previous operation are an admission of failure. Patients must be made aware that several operations may be required before they embark upon a course of treatment.

The accepted 5% to 10% failure rate for microvascular free transfer may be entirely unacceptable to the patient, as may the donor site defect which is wrongly all too often minimized by the surgeon. The length of operations, hospitalizations, and possible intensive care unit treatment must be outlined. Communication with the patient is essential and specific problems such as those relating to eating, speech, and airway diversion must not be an unpleasant shock in the postoperative phase.

Aesthetic or cosmetic surgery

The problem with referral patterns relating to cosmetic surgery have been mentioned above. It is peculiar to this area as many patients wish anonymity and prefer to answer a magazine advertisement rather than contact their own general practitioner. It was in an effort to distribute unbiased information to doctors and the public, that the organization known as the British Association of Aesthetic Plastic Surgeons (BAAPS) was formed. Through this, doctors may obtain access to lists of trained plastic surgeons in their area.

The complications relating to aesthetic surgery are legion. Examples over recent years are:

1. The umbilicus to one side of the midline after an abdominoplasty.
2. A burn from a hot water bottle to the anaesthetic lower abdomen after an abdominoplasty.
3. Blindness after blepharoplasty.
4. Facial paralysis after facelift, usually either the mandibular or frontal branches of the facial nerve being damaged.
5. Breasts considered too small after breast augmentation.
6. Breasts considered too large after breast reduction.
7. Unacceptable scars (to the patient) after breast reduction.
8. Death after anaesthetic complications relating to a facelift.

Specific complications for each procedure would be too numerous to list but there are some obvious pitfalls.

Blepharoplasty

Over-zealous removal of orbital fat may cause a 'hollow socket' appearance. If too much skin is removed from the lower eyelid, ectropion may result. Failure adequately to perform haemostasis or to pay heed to postoperative orbital pain can cause pressure on the optic nerve leading to optic atrophy and blindness. Carrying incisions too far medially or laterally may cause webbing or scarring.

Facelifts and neck (platysma) tucks

The facial nerve is particularly at risk in its superficial courses, over the zygoma, in the frontotemporal region and below the mandible. Haematoma may cause skin necrosis. Poor planning may result in asymmetry and loss of the natural angle between the lobe of the ear and the cheek.

Rhinoplasty

'Ski jump' noses, 'saddle' noses, noses with blobby tips, crooked noses, and irregular bony bridges are but some of the complications. It is a difficult procedure which must be carried out only by the experienced practitioner. Even in the best hands postoperative haemorrhage or infection may occur in about 1%. The surgeon and patient must have a clear concept of the balance between what is desired and what is possible, in order to avoid postoperative disappointment. 'Off the shelf' designs are a media creation and bear no relation to what is actually feasible.

Breast surgery

Some problems have been listed above. In breast augmentation some reaction to the silicone prosthesis is common. It is lessened by subpectoral implantation but even then a capsule may form which necessitates removal and reinsertion of the prosthesis. Again, experience is essential. The author has seen a patient with one prosthesis subpectoral and the other sub-mammary due to the incompetence of the occasional operator. In breast reduction newer methods have almost rendered nipple necrosis a thing of the past. However, altered nipple sensation, either reduced or hypersensitive, and an inability to breast feed are common. The patient must be warned of delayed healing at suture junction points and of the possibility of hypertrophic or keloid scars. Breast reconstruction has become more complex due to the variety of methods available. The patient is often well informed and good preoperative counselling is essential.

Prominent ear correction

As a concept this is apparently a simple operation. In reality, it is difficult to achieve a reliable, good result which has the appearance of a natural ear. Sharp cartilaginous folds, a persistent prominence of the upper pole of the ear or of the lobule or even of both (unkindly called a telephone ear) can occur. Problems with the postauricular scars are rare, but as in any anatomical area a keloid scar may result.

Abdominoplasty

Some complications have been mentioned above. A competent plastic surgeon should not run into difficulties relating to umbilical misplacement or skin necrosis. The patient must be aware of the occasional need for a vertical lower abdominal scar. The lateral cutaneous nerve of the thigh must be avoided on each side. Unusual complications such as a lifting forward (usually temporary) of the genitalia must be mentioned.

Liposuction

This is not a method of losing weight. It can only be aimed at treating localized areas of fat such as those in the upper lateral thighs, waistband, lower abdomen, knees, ankles and upper arms. Performed incompetently it can result in unsightly furrowing and an inadequate removal of fat. Shock and fat embolus have been described.

Scar revisions, pock marks, etc.

There are many other areas of aesthetic surgery which involve minor surgical operations. It is probably in this area that most complaints will be received. A naevus or a scar cannot be removed without leaving a scar. The patient must appreciate the balance between what is required and the cosmetic appearance of the result. The back, the presternal area and the deltoid area are all notorious for producing disappointing scars which are either broad, hypertrophic or even keloidal. The injection of pock marks or depressed scars with collagen has not been so successful as was first suggested, and it is now well recognized that repeated injections at three to six monthly intervals are required. Obviously the patient must be made aware of these shortcomings.

Medical reports and evidence

Much of the information required by solicitors from a plastic surgeon revolves around the severity of scarring or deformity, the loss of function, and the likelihood of these being improved by time or surgery. In preceding chapters detailed advice is given on the preparation of reports. Photographs of scars are often disappointing unless taken by a professional photographer experienced in this field. Diagrams with measurements and comments (including the date of the examination) are more helpful.

In court the plastic surgeon will often be in the role of expert witness and subjected to little more than reiteration of the report with clarification of some points. Less often, the surgeon may be pressed to comment on specific treatments and one must be ready to recognize differing opinions between specialists. Ultimately one must rely on the phrase 'in my experience'.

There is a tendency for solicitors to request an estimate regarding the cost of private treatment for scars or other injuries. This must not be treated as a professional referral. The patient must be referred through his general practitioner, or, at the very least, the general practitioner must be made aware of the proposed treatment before it is carried out.

In the unfortunate event of finding oneself as the defendant in a civil action, then the importance of having adequate records becomes readily apparent. Many actions can be short-circuited by prompt discussion with a dissatisfied patient. Mistakes can happen and apologies cannot be construed as admission of guilt. All too often it is a breakdown of communication between doctor and patient, or a misunderstanding on the part of the patient, which is the root cause of the action.

Conclusion

Many areas have not been covered, as they occur but rarely in the average plastic surgical practice. Fetal surgery raises huge ethical questions regarding the balance between treatment of an essentially cosmetic deformity, such as a cleft lip, and the potential life risk to the fetus. Sex change operations, of which there are few performed, raise legal questions such as those concerning registered sex at birth and the subsequent desire to marry after the sex change. The possibility, albeit a fanciful one at present, of facial transplant should keep solicitors busy for years. It is sufficient to say that if plastic and reconstructive surgery continues to change at a rate similar to that of the last decade, we should face an interesting challenge of fresh medicolegal problems in the future.

References

Faulder, C. (1985) *Whose body is it? The troubling issue of informed consent*, Virago Press

Tempest, M. N. (1987) Is the policy of informed consent in the interest of the surgeons or the patient? *British Journal of Plastic Surgery*, **40**, 445–450

Ward, C. M. (1988) Some ethical and legal aspects of plastic surgery. *Journal of the Medical Defence Union*, Spring issue, 10–11

Whitaker, L. A., Munro, I. R., Salyer, K. E., *et al.* (1979) Combined report of problems and complications in 793 Craniofacial operations. *Plastic and Reconstructive Surgery*, **48**, 533

10 Hand surgery

W. B. Conolly

Communication with the patient

Patient's expectations of results from surgery in both trauma and reconstructive surgery have increased greatly in recent years, so that on occasions the impossible is expected. It is important to explain early on why their expectations are not realizable so that dissatisfaction and disappointment can be avoided. For example, patients who arrive in emergency units with amputated parts expect them to be replanted, not realizing that it may not be feasible or, even when feasible, not in their best interests.

Table 10.1 Common reasons for complaints against the doctor by patients with problems

(1)	Failure of doctor to communicate (especially after a bad result), causing resentment, 'Doctor too busy to talk'
(2)	To prevent it happening to others
(3)	For vengeance or money
(4)	To relieve guilt by blaming the doctor, especially in cases of injury of a child
(5)	Pressure from others
(6)	Criticism of doctors by doctors

Missed or delayed diagnosis

It is reasonable to expect that any doctor involved in treating patients with limb injuries should by standard history, physical examination and X-ray be suspicious of divided tendons, nerves and vessels in open injuries; of fractures and joint injuries in closed injuries; of impending congestion and ischaemia in crushing injuries; and the possibility of foreign bodies after puncture wounds by thorns, splinters or glass. If that doctor is in doubt he should ask a more experienced person for advice, make a telephone consultation and/or review that patient within a day or so.

Table 10.2 Medical malpractice case: examples in the hand and upper limb

	The condition	The damage	The negligence	The result
(1)	Glass laceration of forearm Wound sutured Later developed bleeding and Volkmann's contracture	Stiff hand Many operations for contracture	Failure to X-ray and explore and remove the glass foreign body	Settlement out of court for the plaintiff
(2)	Crush injury to three fingers in a farm accident Subsequently developed gangrene and had amputation of the fingers	Loss of fingers Pain and suffering	Failure to remove the dressing when the patient complained of persistent pain	Case successfully defended because the injury alone was sufficient to cause gangrene and loss of the fingers

The diagnosis of damage in an injured hand can be difficult, especially in the case of partial severence of tendons or nerves, and definitive diagnosis can sometimes only be made by formal operative exploration.

A common missed diagnosis is still the fractured scaphoid bone, in spite of its notoriety. In wrist injuries scaphoid views must be specifically requested when arranging an X-ray and if these appear normal, a further X-ray must be arranged two weeks later. Where either of these has been omitted, the case becomes very difficult to defend.

Poor management

This may involve operating on the wrong finger (e.g. trigger finger) or hand (carpal tunnel syndrome), or involve operating without proper facilities such as an adequate and safe tourniquet, adequate anaesthesia or adequate instruments for internal fixation of fractures.

Postoperative management of limb surgery is easily observed and, by and large, well understood by the average patient. He may not understand what is going on in his abdomen after abdominal surgery, but he will know if a plaster is too tight, if a limb is numb, or the deformity has not been corrected.

Tight plasters can be a problem. The surgeon may feel that splitting it may cause loss of position in an unstable fracture, and that some temporary swelling distally, in a limb with good circulation, is acceptable. It is, however, very important to explain to the patient why he must put up with the discomfort of the tight plaster so that he does not consider that it has simply been neglected. In these circumstances good note taking is essential. Complications arising from tight or poorly applied plasters are difficult to defend.

In the management of limb trauma generally, observation of the circulation distally is so important that one would not have thought it could be neglected. However, it is, and rarely can be defended.

Fractures that slip out of position whilst in plaster are an acceptable complication and can be defended, although patients frequently suspect that 'it should not have happened'. The most common culprit in this regard is the Colles fracture.

Another common problem is lack of specialist experience. No doctor should become involved in the repair of tendons, nerves or bones unless he or she has been trained, and has experience, to do so. These patients should be referred on to another person.

The forgotten tourniquet is never defensible.

Inappropriate delegation

A consultant should not delegate a procedure to his or her registrar unless he knows that registrar has sufficient experience for that particular procedure, and unless he, as the consultant, is available for consultation during that procedure.

Complications of surgery

These include iatrogenic damage such as the accidental cutting of a nerve during operation. This may be defensible, as in fasciectomy for Dupuytren's contracture where normal anatomy is distorted, provided all the due precautions of adequate anaesthesia and an avascular field are followed.

Postoperative complications

These are common after hand operations. However, postoperative ischaemia, haematoma, infection and pressure sores rarely occur in the absence of pain. It could be negligent not to remove the dressing and inspect the wound and if necessary,

Table 10.3 Example of summary of facts in a negligence case: case Drs G. and S. concerning the patient Mr G

Date	Time since injury	Condition	Treatment	By whom	Other information	'Accepted' treatment
21.3.86	0	Crush to left hand and index finger	Wounds of hand and index finger sutered LA	Dr S		X-ray Avoid suture
22.3.86	1 day	Blood soaked bandage Swelling of hand and index finger	Antibiotics	Dr G	Pain Swelling Warm	Remove sutures Antibiotics Splint Elevate
24.3.86	3 days	Improvement	Continue antibiotics	Dr G		
27.3.86	6 days	Wounds healed	Sutures removed	Dr G		
5.4.86	15 days	Pain left index finger no sign of infection	X-ray	Dr G		
7.4.86	17 days	Left index finger swollen and deformed	Referred to Dr C	Dr R	X-ray ✚ prox phalanx	
9.4.86	19 days	X-ray showed ✚ ✚ Prox phalanx	Open reduction and internal fixation	Dr C		
?.10.86	6 months		Removal of plate screws			
?.01.87	10 months	Good hand function index finger fails 25 degrees at pip joint				

remove sutures if a patient complained of persistent throbbing pain after a hand operation.

Postoperative joint stiffness is a more difficult issue. This and reflex sympathetic dystrophy are sometimes unpredictable and all one can do is to take the necessary precautions of elevation and dressing change, frequent examinations and assessments, and the encouragement of appropriate exercises at the appropriate time.

It should be pointed out that any complication involving the hand or face remains obvious to the patient and those around him or her.

It is important to warn the patient preoperatively of possible postoperative problems, but the courts accept that, where a risk is very slight, the doctor is not bound to warn of that risk and add to the patient's worries. In implant surgery the patient should be warned of the possibility of implant failure or loosening. It is also wise to discuss the possibility of infection, and what the failsafe procedure might be. Residual disability should be discussed.

In cosmetic surgery, any postoperative complication is viewed with suspicion and, in this surgery, above all other, warnings should be spelled out in detail. Preoperative photographs are often useful to remind the patient later of the preoperative situation with which he or she was previously unhappy.

In hand surgery, a successful outcome depends not just on the doctor's competence but on the patient's cooperation and motivation. Unless the patient can maintain protection of the hand with appropriate elevation and exercises to minimize swelling and stiffness, he or she runs the risk of a poor result. Most patients who sue, complain that their doctor has not told them what their treatment entails and what the result may be. For instance, it is wise to say that about 10% of patients having carpal tunnel decompression may not be relieved of all their symptoms. One-quarter to one-third of patients having flexor tendon repair in the finger may have a degree of stiffness. One third of patients having fasciectomy for Dupuytren's contracture may develop a recurrence of the condition in that hand.

In emergency surgery there may be no time, or it may not be appropriate, to discuss the details of different treatment techniques and their results. In elective surgery, there is always time for such discussion.

11 Anaesthetics
B. J. Lamont

Nightmares
Reality
    Problems associated with general anaesthesia
    Regional anaesthesia
    Drugs
    Children
    Informed consent
    Professional relationships
Sweet dreams
    Standards of current anaesthetic practice
    Audit
    Outcome

This section outlines some common problems which the practice of modern anaesthesia may present for the anaesthetist and the patient. Many of these problems stem from disease processes unrelated to the proposed surgery. These problems can be identified and analysed, using a system of confidential reporting for critical incidents. Adopting new recommendations for minimal monitoring standards may further lower the morbidity and mortality rates associated with anaesthesia.

Nightmares

In the Medical Defence Union Annual Report for 1989, there were five cases cited for claims in the practice of anaesthesia. As an indicator of current practice, three of these are discussed briefly.

Case 1: Disconnection of anaesthetic circuit during surgery

There was no disconnect alarm on the anaesthetic ventilator, and apparently no pulse oximeter attached to the patient. After a time the patient was noted to be peripherally cyanosed and apnoeic; despite resuscitation, death occurred some days later. The case was settled for £9 000.

Case 2: Halothane toxicity?

A sixty-two year old alcoholic patient developed fatal hepatic necrosis after three halothane anaesthetics had been administered in twenty-one days. The cause of death was recorded as 'natural', but the coroner commented on the deleterious effects of closely-spaced halothene anaesthetics. No claim for damages was made.

Case 3: Dental damage

Dental damage was noted in a patient (with poor dentition and a difficult airway) after general anaesthesia for facial surgery. A claim was settled, with no admission of liability, for a small sum as it was felt that the anaesthetist had not appropriately advised the patient of potential damage prior to the anaesthetic.

A claim was settled in a similar case, where an anaesthetic registrar had damaged a crown during intubation, as no prior warning had been given to the patient and no dental guard had been used.

Reality

Problems associated with general anaesthesia

The airway

The major problems in anaesthesia relate to the airway. This seems strange, considering that airway management is one of the prime functions of the anaesthetist.

Unsuccessful intubation of the trachea frequently leads to death. Failure adequately to oxygenate the patient before and during the attempted intubation, is implicated. In the majority of cases, where a normal airway is involved, achieving intubation may become an obsession. A failed intubation 'drill' should be agreed within each anaesthetic department and should be assiduously followed. Auscultating the chest (to confirm successful intubation) can be misleading, as air ventilated into the oesophagus can mimic breath sounds in the chest. The end-tidal carbon dioxide (E_tCO_2) monitor will confirm the presence or absence of CO_2 in the airway. For this reason alone, this monitor may soon be mandatory in American anaesthetic practice.

Other airway problems encountered are obstruction (due to tumour or abnormal anatomy) and the development of bronchospasm.

The next ('technical') problem is disconnection of the oxygen supply to the paralysed patient. Disconnection (or failure of the anaesthetist to transfer the patient from manual to mechanical breathing) was not uncommon with earlier, less-sophisticated ventilators. Disconnect alarms should now be standard fittings on all anaesthetic machines.

Failure to remove throat packs is a real problem. A clear system for retrieval of therapeutically-placed packs should be practised in each operating room.

Absence makes the heart . . .

A hidden problem in the past has been the absence of the anaesthetist from the operating theatre, while a patient is under general anaesthesia. This should *never* occur. Unfortunately, a review of the recent literature reveals an alarming report:

A barrister writing in *The Lancet* described claims that a patient had died under anaesthesia, because the anaesthetist had left the room to have a quick cup of coffee (see Brahams, 1988).

Such situations are rare. While it would be unfortunate to think that work practices force doctors to grab refreshments 'on the run', instead of taking reasonable breaks between procedures, there can be no excuse for exposing anaesthetized patients to such enormous hazards.

Positioning injuries

Nerve damage due to improper positioning is a common reason for medical litigation. The principal cause of the majority of peripheral nerve injuries in anaesthetized patients is ischaemia of the intraneural vasa nervorum (see Britt *et al.*, 1983). This results primarily from stretching of the nerve, and secondarily from compression of a nerve already made vulnerable by stretching. Compression and stretching are likely to occur in the anaesthetized patient as muscle tone is reduced and the patient cannot complain of a postural insult.

The brachial plexus is the most susceptible of all nerve groups to damage from malpositioning during surgery; stretching is the usual cause of injury. Trauma to the circumflex nerve can occur if the bar of a screen presses against the outer aspect of the upper arm. The ulnar nerve may be pinched in the same way if the elbow slips against a hard object during a long procedure. Extreme external rotation of the hips in the lithotomy position can damage the sciatic nerve. The supraorbital nerve can be compressed between the anaesthetic circuit tubing and the bony forehead unless padding is used. Injuries to the facial nerve and to its buccal branch have been caused by undue pressure from a mask or a retaining strap.

Corneal abrasions may occur if the eyelids of the anaesthetized patient are not secured, especially when the head is covered with drapes during the procedure. Chemical injury can be caused by surgical skin wash splashing into the unguarded eye.

Care should be taken when positioning the patient for surgery in the prone position; areas under pressure should be appropriately padded. Even well-designed headrests can cause significant blistering to the face, unless obsessive attention is directed to possible pressure points. Pressure against the eyeball can cause thrombosis of the central retinal artery.

Attention to the positioning (and the duration of inflation) of a tourniquet in limb surgery is important. While injury to the surface area under the cuff seldom results, the inflation time should be recorded and incorporated in the patient's chart. Routine maintenance of the gauges of tourniquets should include accuracy testing.

Arthritis

Surgery is extensively employed for patients suffering from varying degrees of arthritis. Such operations may be major procedures and are frequently prolonged.

The general condition of arthritic patients can be poor; co-existing anaemia is common. Bony abnormalities may contribute to difficulties with placement of intravenous lines and safe positioning of the patient for surgery. Endotracheal intubation may be hazardous in the presence of an unstable cervical lesion, as permanent damage may result from a less-than-skilled attempt at passing an endotracheal tube. Fibreoptic placement of the tube using a local anaesthetic block allows neurological assessment of the patient *after* the tube is safely positioned.

Long periods of immobility on a firm operating table may cause the development of pressure areas or flexion deformities. These problems should be anticipated and preventive measures (extra pillows, the padding of pressure points, flexion of the table, the use of a heated, ripple mattress) should be employed.

Regional anaesthesia

A knowledge of the safe doses of local anaesthetic agents is a prerequisite to their use for regional nerve blocks. It should be noted that the problems associated with the use of these drugs often need correction by a person with specific skills, such as intubation. While a surgeon may have this training, it may not be easy for him to stop a surgical procedure to treat the patient for a complication of the local anaesthetic. Monitored anaesthetic care (whereby an anaesthetist administers the local anaesthetic and monitors the progress of the patient), is safer for the patient, and allows the surgeon to concentrate on the surgical procedure.

Nerve root damage associated with therapeutic nerve blocks has been described. Other specific problems may develop. During spinal anaesthesia, the development of a total spinal blockade must be watched for, and recognized by the anaesthetist. Because the nerves controlling the muscles of respiration may be involved in a high block, cessation of spontaneous respiration due to paralysis of these muscles may occur. Immediate intubation and mechanical support of the respiratory system are critical to the safe recovery of the patient. It follows that only persons trained in the skill of safe intubation should perform spinal anaesthesia.

Hypovolaemia must also be anticipated and avoided. Both these complications may be seen with epidural anaesthesia, if the catheter migrates into the spinal space prior to a 'top-up' of local anaesthetic agent. This is a rare occurrence and, if recognized by the person giving the drug and treated promptly, the complications can be averted.

Anaesthesia of the brachial plexus of nerves can be accomplished by different techniques. Each technique has defined side-effects and complications.

To illustrate this point, consider the possible consequences of a brachial plexus block using the interscalene approach. A known side-effect of this block is the development of a Horner's syndrome, due to involvement in the block of the relevant preganglionic sympathetic fibres which usually leave the spinal cord in the anterior root of the first thoracic spinal segment. This condition reverts to normal with no treatment after the local anaesthetic drug has worn off. Indeed this sign is associated with accurate placement of the drug and the development of a successful block.

Inadvertent injection (by the same approach) of the local anaesthetic drug into the spinal canal can cause the development of a high spinal anaesthetic, with cessation of spontaneous respiration. (This may require treatment as previously described.) In time this block will wear off and the patient may be safely extubated, with no long-term sequelae.

Using the supraclavicular approach for a brachial plexus block, it is possible to cause a pneumothorax or, rarely, damage to the pleura. A chest X-ray can be taken after the procedure to outrule this, but the volume of air introduced into the pleural cavity is rarely significant.

A digital nerve block is useful for some wounds of the finger. Its dangers have been over-emphasized, often without reference to the technique employed. Good safe anaesthesia can be achieved when a knowledge of the anatomy is used. The common volar digital nerves bifurcate at (or near) the distal palmar crease at the level of the metacarpophalangeal joints. A dose of 2 ml of local anaesthetic solution (without adrenaline) is injected carefully into the region of the digital nerve, proximal to the base of the finger, taking care to avoid injection into the flexor tendon sheath. No undue tension, which might interfere with the vascular supply to the digit, is created by this method.

It should be noted that gangrene of the finger can occur if local anaesthetic solution is infiltrated around the base of the finger. The pressure caused by such solutions (even in the absence of adrenaline) can be sufficent to compromise the digital arterial blood supply. A stark photograph of such a complication can be found in one of the standard texts on hand surgery (see Rank *et al.*, 1973).

Complications of local anaesthetic agents can also be due to their rapid systemic uptake which causes toxic levels to develop, effecting excitation of the central nervous system and myocardial depression. (The convulsions seen with overdosage are due to *depression* of inhibitory pathways to motor areas, and consequent over-activity of these centres.)

Different side-effects can be caused by the *same* drugs used for *different* techniques. Thus, in spinal anaesthesia, lignocaine can be associated with the development of an high spinal blockade. It can cause convulsions if it leaks acutely from a regional intravenous anaesthetic (*Bier's* block) into the systemic circulation. Treatment of these complications is very different, and is governed by the basic rules of resuscitation, namely airway management and support of the cardiorespiratory system.

In regional anaesthesia, the possibility of the development of any side-effect is a real one, and must be a factor in the choice of technique to be employed for an individual patient. Facility to intubate *rapidly*, the availability of *effective* suction, an *appropriate* oxygen delivery system and *knowledgeable* assistance are the *minimal* safety precautions required when regional anaesthesia is being performed. It is the duty of the anaesthetist, and the responsibility of the local hospital authority, to ensure that these facilities are available.

(Note that the adverbs and adjectives employed in this

description are the key words to the provision of a safe service for patients, and are often the only distinction between a dangerous and a safe work area.)

Drugs

Halothane

Halothane hepatitis is an uncommon diagnosis as alternative drugs are now available. The use of halothane is usually confined to children and adults presenting for their first anaesthetic or to those who specifically require its characteristic properties.

The 'pill'

Some of the group of anovulant medications are associated with a slight risk of the development of deep venous thrombosis (DVT) in women undergoing surgery. There are two points of view among anaesthetists regarding women on the pill. The first is that no elective surgery should be performed if a woman is taking such a medication; the surgeon should inform the patient of this view at the first meeting. If, however, the patient presents for surgery, she is sent home and given a return date for four weeks after she has stopped the medication.

The second view is that provided the surgery is planned to be short, uncomplicated and followed by full ambulation, there is no need to interfere with the medication. The patient is advised about the risk and of the methods of minimizing the risk, which are early ambulation, anti-embolic stockings and low-dose heparin, where appropriate. This view would consider that the risk of an unexpected pregnancy could have more real consequences for a woman than the small risk of developing DVT.

Anti-depressants

It is common practice to advise patients to discontinue monoamine oxidase inhibitors (MAOIs) and tricyclic anti-depressant (TCADs) drugs for a defined period prior to anaesthesia for elective surgery: four weeks for MAOIs and two weeks for TCADs. Both these groups of drugs interfere with the enzyme systems responsible for catecholamine and neurohormonal breakdown. This withdrawal of medication should be in consultation with the doctor responsible for their prescription. Psychiatrists can often change medications to simpler anxiolytics or other anti-depressants for a short period of time, to allow surgery to be performed.

Children

Children should be met before the planned procedure in the company of their parents. Most attention should be directed to the child in explaining, very simply, what is about to happen. Any alarming details or unpleasant and difficult choices (like 'gas or needle?') should be avoided. The word 'click' *sounds* less painful than 'scratch'. There is now available a cutaneous local anaesthetic (an eutectic mixture of local anaesthetic) which gives real anaesthesia for *i.v.* injection if applied to the skin 45–60 minutes before surgery.

Take into account any preferences of the child and parents, but plan the most appropriate technique for each patient. Parents should usually understand that the doctor, after consultation with them, will make the final decision on the type of anaesthetic to be administered.

Informed consent

Undergoing minor surgery has been likened to entering a minefield to buy an ice-cream; it is not without *some* risk. The risks involved in such surgery are fortunately rare. However unlikely the patient is to 'step on a mine', the likelihood of stepping on a second mine would be (after Oscar Wilde) 'downright careless!'

The concept of 'informed consent' implies a discussion of the recommended anaesthetic plan, and its possible complications, with the patient prior to surgery (Lunn, 1988). The plan should conform to a standard of care which is accepted as proper by a body of skilled and experienced medical professionals. Taking the view of the 'lay person', some courts in the United States favour the complete disclosure of *all* information that is reasonably related to a patient's decision. This has been interpreted to extend further the disclosure of facts to include the possibility of many rare complications, which (if occurring together in a bizarre scenario) could contribute to the untimely death of the patient from a simple surgical procedure.

It would seem reasonable, in the interest of the patient and the doctor, to propose (prior to a procedure) a simple plan for therapy, reasonable alternatives to that plan and the potential problems and risks of each. Recent awards by medical litigation assessors would suggest it is wiser to err on the side of over-disclosure.

It is the duty of the anaesthetist to obtain informed consent for anaesthetic procedures; it will be his responsibility to the patient to ensure that no side-effects occur, and that unwanted effects are treated appropriately. Thus an epidural performed by an anaesthetist for analgesia in labour, and for a subsequent Caesarean section operation, would be the responsibility of that anaesthetist.

Professional relationships

At all times, the successful outcome of the proposed surgery is the goal of the surgeon and the anaesthetist. The anaesthetist is an equal professional with joint and independent responsibility for the patient. Normally, neither one controls nor directs the activities of the other. This is the ultimate test of maturity of one professional in cohesion with another. This maturity may occasionally require a demonstration of growth and professional trust. An emotional or adversarial relationship may require modulation by one's professionalism within the framework of a team providing health care. Teamwork should be more than a group of people working together in name only; there should be a common goal. Any conflict should be faced before a procedure is begun. If, as can happen, this is not possible, the responsibility of the anaesthetist must be solely for the benefit of the patient. Patient safety reigns supreme.

Sweet dreams

Standards of current anaesthetic practice

The specialty of anaesthesia involves the physiological manipulation of the cardiorespiratory and central nervous systems by the administration of potentially lethal drugs. Surgery and other invasive procedures may be performed on anaesthetized patients who are maintained on life-support systems until such procedures are completed. The patient is then restored to a state of physiological equilibrium and, hopefully, onto the pathway of least resistance to full recovery.

Thus, anaesthesia in itself is usually not therapeutic. (This is reaffirmed in a recent editorial (*Anesthesia and Analgesia*, 1989), which comments on the *therapeutic* use of thoracic epidural in patients with severe angina.) Any mishap is usually regarded as an unwanted effect, and places the anaesthetist at the forefront of medicolegal risk.

The specialty of anaesthesia has developed from the middle nineteenth century with the discovery that ether induced a state of unconsciousness, a state such that surgical procedures could be performed on people without their awareness of it.

The early years were slow. Despite the use of various other inhaled substances, the application of the newfound art was often unskilled and non-scientific. (There were some notable exceptions. In the 1840s during his brief professional lifetime, John Snow was interested enough in patient outcome to publish two books about his experiences with anaesthetics; he tried to modify his administrations of ether and chloroform by referring to recorded facts of previously administered anaesthetics.)

One of the pioneers of American anaesthesia, Emanuel 'Mannie' Papper recently described the common practice in the 1930s of patients' relatives, porters and various other people pouring chloroform or ether on an unsuspecting individual, to make a surgical procedure painless (see Papper, 1989).

Indeed, this chequered history can be seen characterized in the attitude to anaesthesia of some older clinicians who, having 'passed gas' under similar circumstances in the formative years of training, were persuaded to change to the more developed specialties of internal medicine and surgery.

The development of adequate educational and training facilities for anaesthetists, the manufacture of appropriate equipment and drugs, the surge in published research and knowledge have all led to a revolution which has transformed anaesthesia into its modern intelligent form; capable of providing acute medical care for critically-ill patients.

With such advances, surgical procedures can be performed more safely on people who would have been previously considered too old or too ill for such therapy. Thus, it is mandatory for the anaesthetist at all times to employ a technique with which he or she is familiar, and to be aware of the possible complications associated with that particular approach. Nothing should direct patient management more than good clinical practice. The obligation on the physician should be the provision of the best possible care under the prevailing circumstances; this is a sensible approach.

To make matters more simple, the law takes as its criterion of good *clinical* practice that which a reasonable person would consider good *sound* practice. It is the duty of expert witnesses to help the court determine standards for the 'reasonable person' to apply. It should be noted that the question of *minimum versus optimum* standards is not usually answered by the courts.

Thus, the safety of the anaesthetized patient should be guaranteed by strict adherence to accepted standards of practice. Fear of criticism of one's medical practice leading to adverse publicity (often as a consequence of litigation), has contributed to the emergence of a style of defensive medicine. A recent editorial in *Anaesthesia* (1989), makes the point that anaesthetists, by virtue of their training, tend to anticipate untoward clinical events and thus already practise a form of defensive medicine. We should not have to fear the criticism that our defensive medicine is not best for our patients.

Audit

> *(definition: to make an official systematic examination of ...)*

The recently published report of a Confidential Enquiry into Perioperative Deaths (CEPOD), set up under the auspices of the Associations of Anaesthetists and Surgeons of Great Britain and Ireland, with the financial backing of the Nuffield Provincial Hospitals Trust and the King Edward's Hospital Fund for London has been described as both courageous and unique (see *Anaesthesia*, 1988). No other profession has audited with such veracity the outcome of its work in this way. While other audits have looked at anaesthetic mortality alone (see Table 11.1), this present publication involves both anaesthetists *and* surgeons.

Deaths occurring within 30 days of surgery in three regions in England during 1986 formed the basis of the report. Ninety-five per cent of consultant surgeons and anaesthetists who were approached agreed to take part in the study, and there was 70% retrieval of data relating to the 4034 deaths from more than half a million operations performed.

The study looked at the effects of sixteen different combinations of the following factors: anaesthesia, surgery, surgical disease and intercurrent disease.

Seventy-five per cent of the deaths were due to disease processes and were not, in any way, affected by the process of surgery or anaesthesia.

The overall mortality was 0.7%. The vast majority of these deaths were in elderly people and were due to a progression of the surgical disease or intercurrent disease. Of the total deaths, 195 were due to errors made solely in the surgical process, a rate of 0.04%.

Anaesthesia, along with the patients' pathological process and surgery, was partly responsible for one death in some 1300 operations. Previous reports had suggested that one death in 10 000 operations was due solely to anaesthesia; these reports failed to implicate surgical factors as causing postoperative complications. Thus, in this report, only three deaths were wholly attributable to anaesthesia, a rate of 0.0005% (one in 185 000).

Seeking to analyse further the factors contributing to mortality (see Lunn, 1988), the study highlighted several areas. Fifteen per cent of patients were not visited preoperatively. Recovery rooms were not always available, and some were closed at night and at weekends because of staff shortages. Inadequate monitoring was reported in 21% of cases.

Table 11.1 Risk of anaesthetic-related death (Cunningham, 1987)

Study	Location	Study period	Published	Risk
Beecher	USA	1948–1952	1954	1 : 2680
Harrison	S Africa	1957–1966	1968	1 : 3068
Marx	USA	1966–1969	1973	1 : 1265
Harrison	S Africa	1967–1976	1978	1 : 4537
Lunn	UK	1981	1982	1 : 10 000
Tiret	France	1978–1982	1986	1 : 8000
CEPOD[a]	UK	1986	1987	1 : 185 000

[a] Anaesthesia partly responsible for 1 : 1300 deaths.

Outcome

In two studies, Cooper et al. (1982, 1984) looked at the reporting of near-misses and cases with substantive negative outcomes (SNOs) and severe patient morbidity or a fatality. (An anaesthetic near-miss is an event occurring during the perioperative time, which has the potential to cause significant harm, but fails to do so because action is taken to abort the event or prevent its conclusion.)

The types of incidences in both studies were similar. The majority of them were due to human error, while a much smaller percentage was due to equipment failure.

Not all near-misses result from gross errors. Some result from subtle errors in vigilance, judgement or technique, some from the patient's condition, and others from true equipment failure. In every anaesthetic department, there should be a system for reporting and analysing these significant events to prevent such errors recurring.

The Recommendations for Standards of Monitoring during Anaesthesia and Recovery, published by the Association of Anaesthetists of Great Britain and Ireland (1988), reflect the universal concern of the specialty to improve patient care and outcome following anaesthesia, and reduce for its members the risk of avoidable litigation.

Such standards for minimal monitoring, as set in America and Canada, specify the continuous presence of the anaesthetist in the operating theatre, the monitoring of heartrate (by ECG) and blood pressure, breathing system disconnect alarms and inspired oxygen concentration analysis. The ability to measure accurately end-tidal CO_2 (allowing real ventilatory control of a patient) and the use of infrared pulse oximetry are also acknowledged as desirable, in a recent report from the Irish Standing Committee of the Association and the Faculty of Anaesthetists in the Royal College of Surgeons in Ireland.

It is hoped that such self-audit will result in a reduction in patient morbidity and in the elimination of iatrogenic mortality, making anaesthesia safer for all.

References

Brahams, D. (1988) Medicine and the Law. *Lancet* **ii**, 3rd September, p. 581

Britt, B., Joy, N. and Mackay, M. (1983) Positioning Trauma. In *Complications in Anesthesiology* (ed. F. K. Orkin and L. H. Cooperman). J. B. Lippincott Co., Philadelphia, pp. 646–670.

Cooper, J. B., Long, C. D. and Newbower, R. S. (1982) Critical incidences associated with intraoperative exchanges of anesthesia personnel. *Anesthesiology,* **56**, 456–461

Cooper, J. B., Newbower, R. S. and Kitz R. J. (1984) An analysis of major errors and equipment failures in anesthesia management: considerations for prevention and detection. *Anesthesiology,* **60**, 34–42

Cunningham, A. J. (1987) Editorial: Anaesthesia in Ireland, How safe is it? *Irish Journal of Medical Science* **156**, (10), iii–iv

Editorial. (1988) A confidential enquiry into perioperative deaths. *Anaesthesia,* 91–92

Editorial. (1989) Anaesthetists, lawyers and the public. *Anaesthesia,* **44**, 1

Editorial. (1989) Is anesthesia therapeutic? *Anesthesia and Analgesia,* **69**, 555–557

Lunn, J. (1988) Mortality studies in the United Kingdom. *Canadian Journal of Anaesthesia,* **35**, 281

Norton, M. L. and Norton E. V. (1986) Legal aspects of anesthesia practice. In *Anesthesia* (ed. R. D. Miller) **21**, 27–50

Papper, E. (1989) In retrospect. *Journal of the American Medical Association,* September 1st, **262**, (9), 1225–1227

Rank, B. , Wakefield, A. and Hueston, J. (1973) *Surgery of Repair as Applied to Hand Injuries.* Churchill Livingstone, Edinburgh, p. 89

12 Otolaryngology
M. R. Hawthorne and A. F. Dingle

As in other medical specialties litigation against practitioners in otolaryngology has been increasing over recent years. Unfortunately, many cases are indefensible due to lack of adequate record-keeping even though negligence may not have occurred. Indications for surgery, details concerning the risks explained to the patients, and progress should be carefully noted. Where there is more than one course of action, the wise practitioner should record any reasons for following the chosen path.

Errors and failures in diagnosis

Litigation in this area is unusual: however, there are several important factors to be considered.

Diagnosis of deafness in young children

Failure to diagnose leads to delayed rehabilitation, which is very important in children under two years. It is important to suspect deafness in high-risk children and when the mother states that the child has a hearing problem. If necessary, objective audiometry should be performed.

Diagnosis of epiglottitis

This should be suspected in pyrexial patients complaining of 'something lodged in the throat' or breathing difficulties.

Diagnosis of a foreign body

A normal radiograph appearance does not exclude the presence of a foreign body. An endoscopic examination should be performed in patients with suspicious symptoms or signs. It should be remembered that partial dentures can be swallowed and that they may not contain radio-opaque material.

Diagnosis of acoustic neuroma

This can be very difficult – not every case presents with the classic neural hearing loss and canal paresis. A brainstem auditory response audiogram and reflex decay should be performed. Any abnormality should alert the otologist to the necessisity of a CT scan.

Diagnosis of a cholesteatoma

Chronically discharging ears that have failed to settle with conservative management, including eradication of sources of sepsis, may harbour a cholesteatoma. Exploration of the ear may be required.

Diagnosis of malignancy

To exclude malignant disease, biopsy is essential in ulcers that fail to heal, post-irradiation oedematous larynges, and persistent fistulae.

Outpatient procedures

In busy outpatient and casualty departments informed consent is often forgotten. Litigation can easily arise from this omission.

Ear syringing

Claims arising from this procedure are the commonest source of litigation in otolaryngology. If the task of ear syringing is delegated, the doctor should ensure that the staff have been adequately trained. It is important that contraindications are identified. The procedure should be painless and irrigation should be stopped at any complaint.

Nasal cautery

Caustics can run down the upper lip, causing skin burns and scarring. Over-enthusiastic cautery may lead to septal perforation. Such an outcome indicates a negligent technique.

Antral lavage

Accurate placement of the cannula is important. There is a risk of injection of liquid into the orbit or subcutaneous tissues. Failure to recognize such a complication immediately may be considered negligent.

Drugs

Cocaine

The administrator of this controlled drug should be aware of the side-effects and symptoms of overdosage. It is difficult to assess accurately dosage of paste. Cardiac arrhythmias are easily induced. Interactions with other drugs, especially beta-blockers, must not be forgotten.

Ototoxic drugs

Short courses of aminoglycoside-containing ear drops are justified as the risk of drug-induced ototoxic damage is less than the ototoxic effects of suppuration. In patients with normal renal function embarking on a course of parenteral aminoglycoside therapy, audiology may be dispensed with provided that blood levels are monitored and the patient claims normal hearing. Patients with reduced renal function or sensorineural hearing impairment should be monitored audiologically and for raised serum drug levels.

Patients undergoing treatment with Cisplatin should be monitored audiologically.

Significant ototoxic risks of any drug therapy should be explained to all patients undergoing such therapy.

Consent

It is the responsibility of the operating surgeon to obtain consent. If this task is delegated to a junior doctor, the surgeon should ensure that all relevant information has been presented to the patient, i.e. all risks that the patient would consider material should be explained, the nature of any potential complications should be explained in full and the patient should be made aware of the possible outcome of his or her disease without surgical intervention. Surgeons should indicate the likely outcome and any risks of a procedure at their hands.

Surgical principles

General risks have been covered in previous chapters, but there are some risks specific to otolaryngology.

Swabs and packs

Following adenoidectomy swabs may be left in the postnasal space. Any dressings left *in situ* post surgery should be recorded lest they not all be removed. Nasal packs should be secured externally as they may be swallowed or inhaled. Insertion of large packs of bismuth iodoform paraffin paste may lead to ingestion of a toxic dose − with resulting confusion.

Bandages

These should not be so tight as to cause pressure necrosis of the soft tissues.

Diathermy

There is a risk of burns, especially in tonsillectomy.

Explosive gases

These should not be used where there is a risk of explosion, for example in submucosal diathermy of the inferior turbinates.

Dental damage

Patients with dental crowns or loose teeth should be identified. Patients undergoing operations involving oral instrumentation such as tonsillectomy or laryngoscopy should be warned of the risks of dental injury.

Blood transfusion

Most surgeons do not warn of the complications of transfusion. In surgery for life-threatening conditions the risks of refusing surgery on the grounds of a blood transfusion complication far outweigh the small chance of such a complication arising. However, tonsillectomy and inferior turbinectomy have an appreciable incidence of major haemorrhage. In this situation the scales may be more finely balanced and consequently some surgeons now mention the possibility of blood transfusion to their patients undergoing surgery for relatively minor conditions.

Laser

In inexpert hands there is a grave risk of injury to patients and staff. A hospital safety policy should be in operation and strictly adhered to. Only hospital-approved surgeons should use laser equipment.

Ear surgery

General principles

An audiometric and clinical assessment of hearing before

surgery should be recorded. In surgery for vertigo, or where there is surgical risk to the inner ear, examination of the vestibular system should be recorded. It is generally accepted in tympanomastoid surgery that a simple clinical examination and history concerning the vestibular system suffices. In inner ear surgery, for example saccus decompression, a more detailed examination including caloric testing of both ears is advisable.

Tympanomastoid and ossicular surgery

The principal risks are loss of hearing, balance, facial nerve function and exacerbation of tinnitus. There is no consensus of opinion as to which patients should be warned of what concerning these factors. In mastoid surgery there is a large body of opinion that all four factors are discussed. Few surgeons would mention the risk of facial paralysis or vertigo in simple myringoplasty as these complications are rare.

It is in the area of ossiculoplasty that the greatest variation in the practice of taking consent occurs: however, in a climate of increasing litigation the wise surgeon should warn of all four possibilities while emphasizing their rarity. Ideally surgeons should give some indication of the percentage risks and likely success at their hands.

Stapedectomy produces a surprising amount of litigation for an operation that is so infrequently carried out, due to the relatively high risk of 'dead ear' with vertigo. Even facial palsy can occur. Research has shown that the complication rates drop with experience of the surgeon. The occasional stapedectomist can expect to be sued and there is, therefore, a growing body of opinion that this operation should be performed by a limited number of surgeons. Some surgeons are now grouping their patients so that several such operations are performed over a few consecutive days.

Following ear surgery any facial paralysis that has not recovered within a few hours demands prompt management. The surgeon with little experience of facial nerve decompression is well-advised to refer the patient to a local expert. In most cases prompt re-exploration of the ear is likely to produce the best result for all concerned. If possible, photographs should be taken of both the patient and the operative findings. Sadly, settlements have frequently been larger than necessary due to delays in the management of this situation.

Iatrogenic facial paralysis may be defended in certain situations, including congenital dehiscence, ectopic site, exposure by disease and biopsy of a middle ear mass that transpires to be a facial neuroma. However, when one of these rare situations is encountered the surgeon should endeavour to have his or her findings verified by a colleague or recorded photographically. Good operation notes must be kept.

Prosthetic failure is fortunately rare. It usually leads to litigation against both the surgeon and the manufacturer. The surgeon may be accused by the manufacturer of handling the prosthesis in such a manner that it failed. Where possible the surgeon should make every attempt to retrieve the prosthesis so that it may be subjected to fault analysis by an independent assessor. Sadly this may not be always possible, for example when a prosthesis falls into the vestibule of the inner ear.

Nose and sinus surgery

General principles

The indications for surgery have to be clearly established and the patient should not have unrealistic expectations. Many patients have such factors as smoking militating against a good surgical result which should be taken into consideration when counselling the patient. Furthermore, symptoms such as nasal stuffiness, 'catarrh' and headaches are very subjective. Prognosis concerning such symptoms should be guarded.

Cosmetic facial surgery is not included in this chapter. Careful psychological assessment of patients requesting such treatment is of paramount importance.

Intranasal surgery is fraught with difficulty because of poor visibility. The orbital contents are at risk, penetration of the intracranial cavity can occur with dire results, ethmoid and turbinate surgery can lead to massive haemorrhage. These complications are fortunately rare and most surgeons in the UK do not warn their patients of them.

In radical surgery for malignant disease of the paranasal sinuses it is usual to warn that the orbital contents may need to be sacrificed, or that sensory deficits and intracranial complications may occur.

Septal surgery

The main areas where litigation can arise are saddle deformity and septal perforation. Barely noticeable supratip depression is common and rarely leads to complaint. Major external deformity and septal perforation are fortunately rare and few surgeons warn against it. Occasionally paraesthesia and black discoloration of the upper incisors occurs. These complications do not imply negligence in surgical technique.

Antral surgery

Sensory deprivation to the teeth, forehead and cheek can occur. Oroantral fistula can occur, but is rarely due to negligence. Few surgeons warn of anything other than sensory aberration of the cheek.

Ethmoid surgery

Most complications arise following the use of an intranasal approach (see above). An external approach minimizes these risks — intranasal ethmoidectomy is not for the dabbler. Risks can be minimized by good illumination, the use of blunt instruments and familiarity with the anatomy.

Functional endoscopic surgery

The orbit and the anterior cranial fossa can be entered easily. In radical ethmoidectomy especially, there is a risk of trauma to the optic nerve; consequently few surgeons use this new technique. A common practice of consent has not yet been established. This type of surgery should *not* be undertaken without adequate training.

Head, neck and throat surgery

General principles

Endoscopy, parotid surgery and thyroid surgery are covered in the chapter on general surgery.

Where the airway is at risk in major neck and pharyngeal surgery a tracheotomy should be performed, or careful postoperative monitoring of oxygen saturation should be undertaken.

In obtaining consent for laryngeal, tongue and palatal surgery the possibility of a voice change should not be forgotten.

Neck surgery for benign conditions

Neural or vascular damage is rarely defensible unless there are adverse surgical conditions such as infection, and then only if adequate consent has been obtained.

At particular risk are the accessory nerve in the posterior triangle, the lingual, hypoglossal and mandibular branches of the facial nerves in the submandibular triangle, the carotid artery and jugular vein. Cricopharyngeal myotomy places the recurrent laryngeal nerve at risk.

The decision to warn against damage to all of these structures should be taken in the light of the pathology, the experience of the surgeon and the surgical conditions. In addition the patient's social and personal factors should be considered.

Neck surgery for malignant conditions

Litigation arising out of radical surgery for cancer is rare, because deliberate section of neural structures is anticipated in advance and warned about. Furthermore, patients with malignant disease accept more readily deficits arising out of radical treatment for life-threatening disease.

Conclusion

Most litigation can be avoided by:

1. Keeping comprehensive and accurate records
2. Keeping the patient informed
3. Confining the patient management to areas with which the otolaryngologist is familiar
4. Never being too proud to ask a colleague for advice.

13 Ophthalmology

D. K. Chitkara and B. J. McNeela

Ophthalmology like other medical specialties has shown an escalating trend in claims for medical negligence in recent years; yet in the league table of surgical claims ophthalmologists are almost at the bottom. Furthermore, the incidence of challenge is only a minute proportion of the total ophthalmic clinical delivery. Yet loss of vision is a highly traumatic experience for the patient, both physically and emotionally. The judgements of the courts reflect this. While it is important not to be complacent, it is equally important to keep a sense of proportion over the relatively small size of the problem.

There are basically two aspects of ophthalmic practice which commonly give rise to a challenge: errors of *execution* and errors of *omission*. This chapter will highlight the common source of error in the two categories.

Errors of execution

Actions resulting from alleged negligence of medical treatment or surgical technique are relatively uncommon. However, certain procedures commonly give rise to complaints:

Perforation of globe

This occurs more commonly than is realized during squint surgery and from retrobulbar injections. Care must be taken during these procedures and failure to recognize perforation is inexcusable.

Laser treatment

The common accidental complications of laser treatment include corneal burns during highly energetic laser treatment and macular burns resulting from 'losing your way as you go around the retina' during pan-retinal photocoagulation.

Subretinal membranes do occur in middle-aged patients and can mimic central serous retinopathy. Inadequate treatment of these will inevitably worsen the underlying pathology.

Lid surgery

One of the common causes for claims is a poor cosmetic result from lid surgery. Removal of large xanthelasma, particularly from lower lids, can give rise to ectropion unless the need for skin grafting is recognized.

Misuse of drugs

One of the common errors in general practice is to prescribe topical steroids without excluding by fluorescein staining the presence of a dendritic ulcer. Patients given topical steroids must be followed-up by ophthalmologists so that the development of geographical ulcers can be avoided.

Errors of omission

Errors of omission far outweigh in frequency and importance all other sources of trouble. The clinical examination of a patient gives many opportunities for omission, which may be related to professional conduct, failure of diagnosis and especially failure of communication.

There are several areas where problems often arise.

Ocular trauma

By far the greatest number of claims still arise from the missed intraocular foreign body. Ophthalmologists are responsible for up to one-third of these; the remainder are accounted for by casualty officers and general practitioners.

The typical circumstances giving rise to this event occur when the patient has been striking metal on metal or using power tools. On examination the small foreign body may not be seen and is then assumed to have fallen off or to have been rubbed off, leaving behind a corneal abrasion over a small, self-sealing wound. The possibility of foreign body penetrating the eye is not considered and X-ray examination of the orbit is not performed.

The most serious complications are severe endophthalmitis and loss of the eye. The diagnosis of retained intraocular foreign body must be considered, particularly if there is history of using a hammer and chisel or power tools. All patients with such injuries must have an orbital X-ray and the posterior segment of the eye should be examined. The message is: *always* X-ray if in any doubt.

Retinal detachment

Medicolegally one of the most problematical groups of cases is missed retinal detachments. Retinal detachment in its early stages can be easily overlooked, especially by the inexperienced examiner, as the symptoms can be vague; yet the results of treatment are closely related to its early detection. In today's climate of high patient expectation, late detection and subsequent poor visual result is understandably seen as grounds for challenge. Retinal detachments can be obscured by vitreous haemorrhage and it is essential that all new episodes of vitreous haemorrhage are examined by ultrasound to exclude this possibility if the fundus is obscured. Although most of the challenges concern missed or late diagnosis of retinal detachment rather than its unsatisfactory surgical management, there is an increasing tendency to question the surgical technique.

Diabetic retinopathy

In developed countries diabetic retinopathy is the commonest cause of registrable blindness in persons under the age of 65 years. Laser photocoagulation has been proven to reduce substantially the risk of serious visual loss, but there are still a large number of diabetic patients who develop severe retinopathy and are referred too late. It is the responsibility of all doctors who care for diabetic patients to ensure that visual acuity and the fundi are checked at least annually by a competent ophthalmoscopist and that the patient is referred if there are signs of significant retinopathy.

Retinopathy of prematurity

The incidence of retinopathy of prematurity has increased in recent years, mainly due to the improved survival of very young and low birth-weight infants. Cryotherapy has recently been shown to be an effective treatment in sight-threatening retinopathy. Ophthalmologists must now become involved in the screening and treatment of at-risk cases, and all neonatal units must ensure that a proper screening programme is set up.

Glaucoma

Misdiagnosis of glaucoma figures less prominently than expected, perhaps due to the wider awareness of the problem and the ease of screening. Certain types of glaucoma, however, need special care.

The first is *steroid-induced glaucoma*. Patients on long-term topical steroid therapy, e.g. for vernal keratoconjunctivitis, must have regular monitoring of intraocular pressure. Failure to diagnose steroid-induced glaucoma with subsequent loss of vision is rarely defensible.

Similarly, a diagnosis of *low tension* glaucoma must be made with caution. This must be fully investigated to exclude optic nerve compression.

Episodes of *subacute angle closure glaucoma* can easily be misdiagnosed as migraine. A careful history and ophthalmic examination will often elucidate the problem once this possibility is considered.

Medical ophthalmology

Temporal arteritis

In any case of rapid visual loss in middle-aged or elderly

patients the possibility of underlying temporal arteritis must be considered. Careful attention to the history, examination and a check on the ESR will avoid preventable visual loss in the second eye.

Malignant hypertension

It is important to check the blood pressure of a patient presenting with any form of vascular insufficiency affecting retinal vessels – approximately 30% of cases of malignant hypertension present with visual symptoms. A missed diagnosis of malignant hypertension can have serious systemic complications in addition to loss of vision. Claims relating to this are difficult to defend.

Systemic drugs

Many systemically administered drugs affect ocular function. Amongst the most serious are ethambutol (used in treatment of tuberculosis) and antimalarials such as hydroxychloroquine (used in treatment of acute rheumatoid arthritis and systemic and discoid lupus). Administration of these drugs is usually started by physicians, but there is much controversy as to the value and cost-effectiveness of screening for their ocular toxicity.

The antimalarials pose a special problem because there is still debate as to whether routine fundal examination and/or tests can detect retinopathy at a reversible or non-progressive stage. Additionally there is the question of who should monitor the vision, – there is a questionable assumption that only ophthalmologists can do this. Nevertheless, retinopathy from the use of antimalarials is very rare provided that the current guidelines on dosage are followed and the patient is made aware of the possible adverse reactions. Perhaps screening is only useful at a research level to help define the safe dose, and so make clinical screening unnecessary.

The visual side-effects of ethambutol are reversible if the

drug is discontinued early. It is therefore essential to recognize this problem at an early stage. Patients should be advised to discontinue therapy immediately if they develop deterioration in vision. Ophthalmologists must remember that a proper history includes an account of the patient's general condition and any drugs being taken.

Laser treatment

With laser treatment patients should be given a full explanation of the possible side-effects. These can be transient — blurred vision due to induced myopia and choroidal detachments, micropsia and raised intraocular pressure — or persistent, with changes in colour vision and visual fields.

Failure of communication

Failure of communication far outweighs in frequency and importance all the other sources of trouble put together. The importance of accurate contemporaneous records cannot be overstated. When records are incomplete or missing, suspicions arise which may damage the defence. In contrast, well-kept medical records may be the first line of defence against alleged negligence. Ophthalmologists are notorious for using abbreviations: only the widely recognized abbreviations should be used.

There must be good communication between the ophthalmologist and patient. Care should be exercised when discussing clinical management with other colleagues in front of the patient. In these circumstances it is easy for an anxious patient to pick up any loose comments, and the seeds of anxiety and loss of confidence may be sown.

The question of informed consent is very much on the agenda for debate. Proper informed consent will help avoid unrealistic expectations, especially where cosmetic surgery is concerned. Of particular significance is the subject of refractive surgery where there is much media hype, but little consensus amongst ophthalmologists. It should be borne in mind that it is easier to explain matters to the patient before a procedure than to a court at a later date.

In the operating theatre it is the responsibility of the ophthalmologist always to identify the patient and the eye to be operated on. If an enucleation is necessary for a malignant melanoma the pupil should be dilated and the fundus checked before surgery. Prior to surgery the muscles to be recessed or resected must be identified. The equipment to be used (e.g. the vitrectomy machine) must also be checked.

The ophthalmologist also has a responsibility when discharging a patient. A patient who develops an endophthalmitis may sue if adequate antibiotic cover was not given. Patients whose pupils are dilated should be warned against driving.

When things do go wrong the ophthalmologist should be careful of what is said to the patient. The patient should be advised of the facts but should never be given excuses, or mere speculation. Criticisms of prior care should be avoided. Good communication will avoid most challenges. It is in this particular direction that our efforts should be directed to raise standards.

Appendix 1

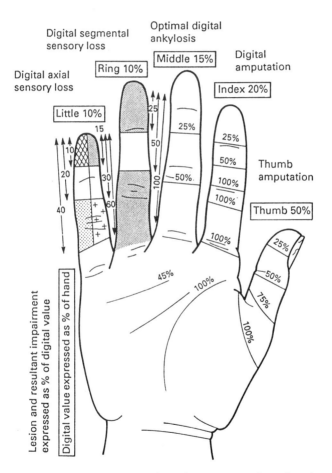

Schematic illustration of a working basis for estimating the order of residual disability subsequent to hand injuries (modified from Rank, Wakefield and Hueston, *Surgery of Repair as Applied to Hand Injuries*, 4th edn, p. 376. Edinburgh, Churchill Livingstone).

Appendix 2

Work available for a one-handed worker

General considerations

1. Dominant or non dominant hand injury.
2. Previous work history. Consider possibility of returning to this with adaptions.
3. Motivation. It is important to consider a report from a Rehabilitation Centre.
4. Consider feasibility of fitting a prosthetic device to assist in re-employment.
5. Is employment influenced by equal employment opportunity legislation or insurance?

'White collar workers'

1. Clerical work including sorting/filing, one-handed typing, keyboard work.
2. Administration.
3. Publicity work.
4. Quality control.
5. Telephonist.
6. Radio/TV worker.

'Blue collar worker'

1. Process work.
2. Conveyor belt operator.
3. Sorting.
4. Quality control.
5. With further training the position of foreman can often be managed, particularly in his pre-accident line of work.
6. Certain driving jobs are possible such as forklift trucks.
7. Security.

Index